Dawat-e-Islami offers this fundam

This book is equally beneficial for non-Muslims who are interested in learning about Islam.

WELCOME TO
ISLAM

(A brief explanation of Islam)

❖

Presented by:

Majlis Al-Madina-tul-'Ilmiyyah

Welcome to Islam

A brief explanation of Islam

❖

ALL RIGHTS RESERVED

Edition:	First
Presented by:	Majlis Al-Madina-tul-'Ilmiyyah (Dawat-e-Islami)
Date of publication:	Ramadan-ul-Mubārak, 1434 AH (Aug, 2013)
Publisher:	Maktaba-tul-Madinah
ISBN:	978-969-579-916-1
Quantity:	10,000

CONTACT

Maktaba-tul-Madinah

Alami Madani Markaz, Faizan-e-Madinah Mahallah Saudagran, Purani Sabzi Mandi, Bab-ul-Madinah, Karachi, Pakistan

✉ E-mail: maktabaglobal@dawateislami.net – ilmia@dawateislami.net

☏ Phone: +92-21-34921389-93 – 34126999

🖷 Fax: +92-21-34125858

اَلْحَمْدُ لِلّٰهِ رَبِّ الْعٰلَمِيْنَ وَ الصَّلٰوةُ وَ السَّلَامُ عَلٰى سَيِّدِ الْمُرْسَلِيْنَ
اَمَّا بَعْدُ فَاَعُوْذُ بِاللّٰهِ مِنَ الشَّيْطٰنِ الرَّجِيْمِ ۚ بِسْمِ اللّٰهِ الرَّحْمٰنِ الرَّحِيْمِ

Du'ā for Reading the Book

Read the following Du'ā (supplication) before you study a religious book or an Islamic lesson, you will remember whatever you study, اِنْ شَآءَاللّٰه عَزَّوَجَلَّ:

اَللّٰهُمَّ افْتَحْ عَلَيْنَا حِكْمَتَكَ وَانْشُرْ
عَلَيْنَا رَحْمَتَكَ يَا ذَاالْجَلَالِ وَالْاِكْرَام

𝒯ranslation

Yā Allah عَزَّوَجَلَّ! Open the doors of knowledge and wisdom for us, and have mercy on us! O the One who is the most Honourable and Glorious!

(Al-Mustaṭraf, vol. 1, pp. 40)

Note: Recite Ṣalāt-'Alan-Nabī once before and after the Du'ā.

اَلْحَمْدُ لِلّٰهِ رَبِّ الْعٰلَمِيْنَ وَ الصَّلٰوةُ وَ السَّلَامُ عَلٰى سَيِّدِ الْمُرْسَلِيْنَ
اَمَّا بَعْدُ فَاَعُوْذُ بِاللّٰهِ مِنَ الشَّيْطٰنِ الرَّجِيْمِ ۙ بِسْمِ اللّٰهِ الرَّحْمٰنِ الرَّحِيْمِ

A Brief Introduction to
Dawat-e-Islami

Dawat-e-Islami, the non-political Movement of Propagation of the Quran and Sunnah is speedily progressing. Dawat-e-Islami has received 'Satisfactory Endorsements' not only from different departments of the Pakistani Government but also from the governments of many other countries as well. There are 98 Jāmi'aat (institutions of higher learning in Islamic studies) for Islamic brothers established in many cities of Pakistan. In addition to this, there are 90 Jāmi'aat for Islamic sisters as well.

More than 75,000 boys and girls are gaining knowledge in Madrasa-tul-Madinah in order to learn Quraanic education i.e. Ḥifẓ and Naazirah (memorization of the Quran and recitation by sight), free of charge. There are Dār-ul-Madinahs whereby both religious and secular education is provided.

اَلْحَمْدُلِلّٰه عَزَّوَجَلَّ, There are also Jāmi'aat in countries other than Pakistan i.e. in India, U.K., Nepal, Bangladesh, Kenya and South Africa.

Besides this, there are many Madani Maraakiz (Centres) which we call Faizan-e-Madinah. The Sunnah inspiring Ijtimaa'āt (Weekly Congregations) and the Bayanāt (Lectures) by Muballigheen

(Preachers) continuously take place. There is a Halqah (Session) of learning and teaching the Sunnah as well as a session of memorizing supplications (Du'ās).

The message of Dawat-e-Islami has reached more than 185 countries of the world. By the mercy of Allah عَزَّوَجَلَّ, Dawat-e-Islami is prospering by day and night. There are more or less 90 departments of Dawat-e-Islami.

It is Almighty Allah's عَزَّوَجَلَّ blessing that the Madani Qaafilas (to spread the Sunnah) are travelling for three, twelve or thirty days, even twelve or twenty-five months. There are a number of Islamic brothers who have dedicated their entire lives to serve the religion of Islam by traveling in Madani Qaafilas.

Madani In'āmaat program: A self accountability program. Simply act upon it on a daily basis for self accountability. You will indeed be inspired by the Madani Ina'āmaat program and would become a well-mannered and practicing Muslim.

It is not less than a blessing if a Muslim gets answers to his Shar'ee (Islamic) questions. اَلْحَمْدُ لِلّٰه عَزَّوَجَلَّ, Dārul-Iftā Ahle-Sunnat is there where Muftis (religious scholars) are making efforts to research and answer the queries of the Muslim Ummah day and night.

Maktaba-tul-Madinah is the publishing department of Dawat-e-Islami. It has the honor to provide the lovers of Rasoolullaah صَلَّى اللّٰه تَعَالٰى عَلَيْهِ وَاٰلِهٖ وَسَلَّم with publishing the books and booklets of Ameer-e-Ahl-e-Sunnat دَامَتْ بَرَكَاتُهُمُ الْعَالِيَه, other Sunni 'Ulamā and of Al-Madina-tul-'Ilmiyyah.

There are websites of at least 8 departments working under the supervision of the IT Majlis. You will be glad to know about Madrasa-tul-Madinah online. The Holy Quran is being taught to hundreds of students within the comfort of their homes through this department, free of charge.

Madani Channel is broadcasted in almost all countries of the world through different satellites and Live Streaming. After watching such a large channel without any females, advertisements and music, several non-Muslims have reverted to Islam.

There is an excellent department called "Jail Khaanajaat". The Islamic brothers of Majlis-e-Jail of Dawat-e-Islami visit jails and train the prisoners within the jails.

Majlis-e-Ta'wizat-e-'Attariyyah is the department which provides thousands of Ta'wizaat (amulets) every month. There is yet another department called "Majlis-e-Ilaaj". This is a department in which thousands of people are associated with Dawat-e-Islami who receive treatment free of charge.

Another department is called "Langar-e-Rizwiyya". Whether it is I'tikaaf, Shab-e-Barā-at, Shab-e-Mi'raaj, Baarwheen Shareef or Ijtimā' of Zikr-o-Na'at, your Dawat-e-Islami serves Langar (meals) to thousands of Islamic brothers. Pakistan was recently affected **badly** with the calamity of earthquakes and by the destructions of **floods**. Dawat-e-Islami worked hard by collecting and distributing **goods and cash, amounting to millions of rupees among affected ones.**

اَلْحَمْدُ لِلّٰهِ رَبِّ الْعٰلَمِيْنَ وَ الصَّلٰوةُ وَ السَّلَامُ عَلٰى سَيِّدِ الْمُرْسَلِيْنَ

اَمَّا بَعْدُ فَاَعُوْذُ بِاللّٰهِ مِنَ الشَّيْطٰنِ الرَّجِيْمِ ۚ بِسْمِ اللّٰهِ الرَّحْمٰنِ الرَّحِيْمِ

Al-Madina-tul-'Ilmiyyah

From:

Shaykh-e-Tariqat Ameer-e-Ahl-e-Sunnat, founder of Dawat-e-Islami, 'Allamah Maulana Abu Bilal Muhammad Ilyas Attar Qadiri Razavi Ziyāee دَامَتْ بَرَكَاتُهُمُ الْعَالِيَه.

Dawat-e-Islami, a global and non-political movement for the preaching of Quran and Sunnah, is determined to revive Sunnah and spread righteousness as well as the knowledge of Shari'ah throughout the world. In order to carry out these great and significant tasks in an excellent way, several Majālis (departments) have been formed including the Majlis 'Al-Madina-tul-'Ilmiyyah' which consists of the 'Ulamā and Muftis of Dawat-e-Islami. This Majlis has ambitiously taken on the responsibility of serving religion in the areas of knowledge, research and publication. It has the following six departments:

1. Department of books of A'lā Ḥaḍrat رَحْمَةُ اللّٰهِ تَعَالٰى عَلَيْه.
2. Department of teaching books.
3. Department of reforming books.
4. Department of translation.
5. Department of scrutiny of books.
6. Department of referencing and documentation.

The topmost priority of Al-Madina-tul-'Ilmiyyah is to present the precious books of A'la Hadrat, Imām-e-Ahl-e-Sunnat, reviver of the Sunnah, eradicator of Bid'ah, scholar of Shari'ah, 'Allamah Maulana Al-Hāj, Al-Qārī, Ash-Shāh Imām Ahmad Razā Khān عَلَيْهِ رَحْمَةُ الرَّحْمٰن in an easily understandable way according to the needs of the present age. All the Islamic brothers and sisters should whole-heartedly cooperate in the development of the Madanī work of knowledge, research and publication, and study every book published by the Majlis as well as persuade others to do the same.

May all the Majālis of Dawat-e-Islami including Al-Madina-tul-'Ilmiyyah progress by leaps and bound ! May Allah عَزَّوَجَلَّ bestow success upon us in the worldly life as well as in the afterlife by enabling us to perform each and every good deed with sincerity! May we all be blessed with martyrdom under the green dome, burial in Jannat-ul-Baqī' and an abode in Jannat-ul-Firdaus.

اٰمِيْن بِجَاهِ النَّبِيّ الْاَمِيْن صَلَّى اللهُ تَعَالٰى عَلَيْهِ وَاٰلِهٖ وَسَلَّم

اَلْحَمْدُ لِلّٰهِ رَبِّ الْعٰلَمِيْنَ وَ الصَّلٰوةُ وَ السَّلَامُ عَلٰى سَيِّدِ الْمُرْسَلِيْنَ
اَمَّا بَعْدُ فَاَعُوْذُ بِاللّٰهِ مِنَ الشَّيْطٰنِ الرَّجِيْمِ ۚ بِسْمِ اللّٰهِ الرَّحْمٰنِ الرَّحِيْمِ

WELCOME TO ISLAM

Faith in Almighty Allah عَزَّوَجَلَّ

To be a Muslim, one has to express his or her firm faith in Towḥeed (the Oneness of Allah عَزَّوَجَلَّ), Most High, and the Prophethood of Prophet Muhammad صَلَّی اللّٰہُ تَعَالٰی عَلَیْہِ وَاٰلِہٖ وَسَلَّم.

Faith in Allah عَزَّوَجَلَّ, the Almighty

Allah عَزَّوَجَلَّ, Most High, is One. There is no partner in His divinity, His works, in His commandments and in His names. Allah عَزَّوَجَلَّ is 'Waajib-ul-Wujood' which means that His existence is necessary at all times. He is Eternal (al-Qadeem) and everlasting (al-Baaqī). None but Allah عَزَّوَجَلَّ, Most High, is worthy of limitless praise and adoration. He عَزَّوَجَلَّ is dependent on no other. On the contrary, everything in the universe is dependent on Him.

The knowledge of Almighty Allah's Being is beyond all imagination and comprehension. It is indeed impossible to comprehend His Supreme Being by using any amount of wisdom, presentation, intellect or intuition because He is beyond imagination, unbound by any limit. It is only possible to imagine something when it has a definite and circumscribed shape or form. But since Allah عَزَّوَجَلَّ, Most High, is formless, unbound and unrestricted, any attempt to visualize Him is impossible. However one can come to know of the existence of Allah عَزَّوَجَلَّ the Most High, through human reason and contemplation of His creations.

Allah عَزَّوَجَلَّ, Most High, is neither a father nor a son of anyone; nor has He any spouse. Those who consider Him as a father or a son are disbelievers.

Allah عَزَّوَجَلَّ, the Most High, all perfections are gathered in Him. He عَزَّوَجَلَّ is pure of all that is impure, defective, cruel, impertinent and indecent. The presence of any drawback and shortcomings in His being is totally impossible.

Telling a lie, deceiving, misappropriation, savagery, ignorance, gracelessness and many other detestable things like these, are absolutely impossible as far as Allah عَزَّوَجَلَّ, Most High, is concerned. Allah عَزَّوَجَلَّ, Most Exalted, is free from all confines of time and space, places and directions, forms and shapes and all those things that resemble any creation.

As far as other Prophets عَلَيْهِمُ السَّلَام are concerned, they saw Allah عَزَّوَجَلَّ, Most High, only in meditations and dreams. It is reported that Imām Abū Hanīfa رَحْمَةُ اللهِ تَعَالَى عَلَيْه, the great Jurist Imām, had the divine vision of Allah عَزَّوَجَلَّ, Most Exalted, more than a hundred times in his dreams.

Allah عَزَّوَجَلَّ, Most High, is the absolute Sovereign: free to do whatever, whenever and however He عَزَّوَجَلَّ Wills. No one can have any control over Him. Nor can anyone distract Him from His intentions. Allah عَزَّوَجَلَّ Most High, neither dozes nor sleeps. He watches over all the worlds. He is never tired, nor is He ever bored. None other than Almighty Allah عَزَّوَجَلَّ is the Preserver of the universe. He is more tolerant, benevolent and loving than parents. His mercy and benevolence provides comfort to broken hearts. All the glories and greatness are but for Him.

Faith in Prophethood

For Muslims, it is essential to know about the Prophets عَلَيْهِمُ السَّلَام and their virtuous qualities as it is essential to know about the supreme Being and the Attributes of Allah عَزَّوَجَلَّ, Most Exalted. It is also essential to have a sound knowledge about Prophethood so that one may avoid wrong notions and misleading beliefs and avoid uttering anything that may amount to degradation of the Prophets عَلَيْهِمُ السَّلَام.

Prophets عَلَيْهِمُ السَّلَام were all men

A Prophet عَلَيْهِ السَّلَام is the person to whom the Divine Revelation from Allah عَزَّوَجَلَّ, Most Exalted, is bestowed for the guidance of mankind. Such a person is also called an Apostle or Messenger of Allah عَزَّوَجَلَّ, Most Exalted.

All the Prophets عَلَيْهِمُ السَّلَام sent by Almighty Allah عَزَّوَجَلَّ, were human beings and men. No woman was ever accorded the status of a Prophet. It was not obligatory for Almighty Allah عَزَّوَجَلَّ, to send His Prophets عَلَيْهِمُ السَّلَام. Nevertheless, out of His extreme kindness He عَزَّوَجَلَّ sent the Prophets عَلَيْهِمُ السَّلَام for the guidance of mankind. A Prophet must receive Waḥī or Divine Revelation whether it is bestowed upon him through Angles or through any other means.

❖ ❖ ❖

The prominent Prophets عَلَيْهِمُ السَّلَام of Almighty Allah

Allah, the Most High, sent down many Prophets عَلَيْهِمُ السَّلَام for the guidance of mankind from the time of Prophet Ādam عَلَى نَبِيِّنَا عَلَيْهِ وَالِهِ وَسَلَّم to Prophet Muhammad صَلَّى اللهُ تَعَالَى عَلَيْهِ وَالِهِ وَعَلَيْهِ الصَّلوةُ وَالسَّلَام. While some of them have been mentioned specifically in the Holy Quran, many others have not figured in it. The Prophets عَلَيْهِمُ السَّلَام who have been given prominence in the Holy Quran are: Prophet Ādam, Prophet Idrīs (Enoch), Prophet Nūḥ (Noah) Prophet Hūd, Prophet Sāliḥ, Prophet Ibrāhīm (Abraham), Prophet Ismāʼīl (Ishmael), Prophet Isḥaaq (Isaac), Prophet Lūṭ (Lot), Prophet Yaʼqoob (Jacob), Prophet Yūsuf (Joseph), Prophet Shuʼaib, Prophet Ayyūb (Job), Prophet Mūsā (Moses), Prophet Hārūn (Aaron), Prophet Dhul Kifl (Ezekiel), Prophet Dāwood (David), Prophet Sulaimān (Solomon), Prophet Zakarīyā (Zecharia), Prophet Yaḥyā (John), Prophet ʻĪsā (Jesus Christ) and the Leader of all Prophets Sayyidunā Muhammad عَلَيْهِمُ الصَّلوةُ وَالسَّلَام.

How many Prophets عَلَيْهِمُالسَّلَام؟

It is not advisable to put an exact figure on the number of Prophets عَلَيْهِمُ السَّلَام sent down by Allah عَزَّوَجَلَّ, the Most Wise, for the guidance of mankind because the opinion on this point differs. The safest way is to believe and say that Allah عَزَّوَجَلَّ sent more or less 124,000 prophets عَلَيْهِمُ السَّلَام.

Faith in Angels

Angels are neither male nor female; neither eat nor drink; neither marry nor reproduce. They are made of light and hence they can change themselves into different forms. They also have the power to transmute themselves into any form but they never do any such thing knowingly or unknowingly against the command of Almighty Allah عَزَّوَجَلَّ.

Every Angel has a specific assignment to accomplish. Some Angels bring Waḥī (Revelation) from Almighty Allah عَزَّوَجَلَّ, to His Prophets عَلَيْهِمُ السَّلَام. Some of them are responsible for the rain while others are responsible for supplying provision to worldly creatures. Some Angels عَلَيْهِمُ السَّلَام shape the face of the fetus in the womb of the mother, while some take care of the changes in human bodies.

Some Angels عَلَيْهِمُ السَّلَام are responsible for providing protection to living beings from their enemies and lurking dangers. Some Angels عَلَيْهِمُ السَّلَام move about to attend the functions and meetings held in remembrance of Almighty Allah عَزَّوَجَلَّ, and His Prophets عَلَيْهِمُ السَّلَام.

Some Angels carry forward the salutations and greetings of Muslims to Prophet Muhammad صَلَّى اللّٰهُ تَعَالَى عَلَيْهِ وَاٰلِهٖ وَسَلَّم while some have been assigned the job of blowing the decisive Ṣoor (Clarion) just before the Day of Judgment.

Sayyidunā Jibrāīl عَلَيْهِ الصَّلٰوةُ وَالسَّلَام is the Archangel. His title is 'Rooḥ-ul-Ameen.' He visited the Holy Prophet صَلَّى اللّٰهُ تَعَالَى عَلَيْهِ وَاٰلِهٖ وَسَلَّم twenty four thousand times, Nabī Ādam عَلَيْهِ السَّلَام twelve times, Nabī Idrīs عَلَيْهِ السَّلَام four times, Nabī Nooḥ عَلَيْهِ السَّلَام fifty times, Nabī Ibrāhīm عَلَيْهِ السَّلَام 42 times, Nabī Ayyūb عَلَيْهِ السَّلَام three times, Nabī Ya'qoob عَلَيْهِ السَّلَام four times, Nabī Mūsā عَلَيْهِ السَّلَام four hundred times and Nabī 'Īsā عَلَيْهِ السَّلَام ten times.

The other prominent Angels are Sayyidunā Mīkā-eel, Sayyidunā Isrāfil and Sayyidunā Izra'eel عَلَيْهِمُ الصَّلٰوةُ وَالسَّلَام. Sayyidunā Izra'eel عَلَيْهِ الصَّلٰوةُ وَالسَّلَام is the Angel of death. Then there are the Angels who are carrying the 'Arsh (Throne) and the Kursī (Chair). The Angels possess no conscience or reason of their own. They are created simply to obey Allah عَزَّوَجَلَّ, the All-Powerful. They never ask questions like why, how and what without the permission of Allah عَزَّوَجَلَّ. They are totally dedicated to the Will of Allah عَزَّوَجَلَّ, the Supreme Creator.

Two Angels are always accompanying man on both the shoulders called 'Kirāman Kātibīn', they are the Scribes. They record the daily account of man's good and bad deeds. The other two famous Angels are 'Munkar-Nakīr'. After burial, these Angels call on the dead and ask three questions pertaining to faith:

1. Who is your Rabb (Lord)?

2. What is your religion?

3. What you used to say about him (referring to the Holy Prophet Muhammad ﷺ)?

The other super-natural creatures are called Jinns (Genies). They are created from fire. Some of them have the power to adapt to any shape they wish. They have very lengthy lives although some of their dimensions, like intelligence and spirits are just like human beings. They eat, drink and procreate and die like humans. There are Muslims as well as non-Muslims amongst the Jinns and to treat all of them metaphorically as evil doers is strictly forbidden.

Faith in the books of Almighty Allah عَزَّوَجَلَّ

All the heavenly books are true and whatever Almighty Allah عَزَّوَجَلَّ has said through them, is to be believed in. However, due to distortions, their originality has been brought into question. The preservation of these Holy Scriptures was entrusted to their respective followers, and rather than preserving the books in their memories and on tablets, the books suffered alterations. The outcome was that these books could not be relied upon to be the same as when they were originally revealed and those who had vested interests altered the words and letters to change the meanings in order to make them conveniently suit their personal interests. They even indulged in addition and deletion in accordance with their whims and fancies. This kind of distortion in respect of the Scriptures is called 'Tahreef'.

It is therefore advisable that when we come across anything mentioned in previous Scriptures, we would accept it only if it is in conformity with the Magnificent Quran. But if it is contrary to the Holy Quran we should deem it to be an outcome of 'Tahreef'. In the case of confusion over a thing being consistent or inconsistent with the Glorious Quran, we should neither accept those things immediately nor should we deny it outright, our stand in such cases should be cautious.

The Glorious Quran, the Last Testament of Almighty Allah عَزَّوَجَلَّ

Almighty Allah عَزَّوَجَلَّ sent down many Holy Scriptures through many Prophets عَلَيْهِمُ الصَّلٰوةُ وَالسَّلَام. Four of them are the most famous:

1. The Taurāt (Torah) revealed to Prophet Mūsā عَلَيْهِ السَّلَام.

2. The Zabūr (Psalms) revealed to Prophet Dāwood (David) عَلَيْهِ السَّلَام.

3. The Injeel (Bible) revealed to Prophet 'Īsā عَلَيْهِ السَّلَام.

4. The Glorious Quran revealed to our Beloved Prophet Sayyidunā Muhammad صَلَّ اللهُ تَعَالٰی عَلَيْهِ وَاٰلِهٖ وَسَلَّم, the Seal of the Prophets.

There is no scope of any superiority or inferiority as far as the Holy Word of Almighty Allah عَزَّوَجَلَّ is concerned. However, the Holy Quran stands out to be the most rewarding.

Death and the grave

Death is when the soul comes out of the body. Everyone has to die. Nothing can save one from death. The time of death is fixed for everyone. Nothing can delay it.

When a person's life is ending, the Angel Izra'eel عَلَيْهِ الصَّلٰوةُ وَالسَّلَام comes to remove the Rooḥ (soul) from the dying person. When the dying person looks to his left and to his right, he sees Angels everywhere. The Angels of Mercy come to a Muslim. The Angels of Punishment come to the Kaafirs (disbelievers). A Muslim's soul is taken out with ease and respect by the Angels of Mercy. A Kaafir's soul is taken out with great pain and disgrace. When someone visits a grave, the souls see the person, recognize him or her and listen to what they are saying. They can even hear the footsteps of the visitors.

What happens after burial?

After the person is buried, the grave tightens up and presses the dead. It presses the Muslim like a mother firmly embraces her child. It squeezes a Kaafir in such a way that the left ribs are crushed and interlock with the right side. When the people leave the burial, the dead person hears the footsteps of the people. At that time, two Angels called Munkar and Nakeer come ripping through the earth with their long teeth. Their faces look very fearful and scary. Their bodies are black in color. They have blue eyes, which are very large in size and popping out of their foreheads. They are fiery. Their hair is very frightful and long from head to toe. Their teeth are also very long with which they rip through the earth. They wake up the dead shaking and rattling them. With great strength and a gruff voice, they ask these three questions:

a. 'مَنْ رَّبُّكَ؟' meaning 'Who is your Lord?'

b. 'مَا دِيْنُكَ؟' meaning 'What is your religion?'

c. 'مَا كُنْتَ تَقُوْلُ فِيْ حَقِّ هٰذَا الرَّجُلِ؟' meaning 'What you used to say about this person?'

If the dead person is a Muslim, he will reply as follows:

a. 'رَبِّيَ اللّٰهُ' meaning 'My Lord is Allah (عَزَّوَجَلَّ).'

b. 'دِيْنِيَ الْإِسْلَامُ' meaning 'My religion is Islam.'

c. 'هُوَ رَسُوْلُ اللّٰهِ' meaning 'He (صَلَّى اللّٰه تَعَالٰى عَلَيْهِ وَاٰلِه وَسَلَّم) is Allah's Messenger.'

Now a voice from the skies will be heard saying: "My servant has spoken the truth. Lay the tablecloth of Paradise for him. Give him clothes from Paradise to wear and open the doors of Paradise (Jannah) for him." The cool air and the sweet fragrance of Jannah will fill the air. The grave will be made wide and large. The Angels will say: "Sleep like a groom sleeps on his wedding night," this will be for the good pious Muslims.

The sinful will be punished according to their sins. This punishment will continue for a time. The punishment can stop when somebody supplicates (makes Duʿā) for the dead person or when Allah عَزَّوَجَلَّ the Most Merciful shows His Mercy to the dead.

If the dead person is a hypocrite (Munafiq), then he will not be able to answer the questions and will say "هَيْهَاتَ هَيْهَاتَ لَا اَدْرِى" meaning "Shame for I know nothing." A caller will shout: "He is a liar, lay the table-cloth of fire for him, and give him clothes of fire to wear and open the doors of Hell for him, for which the heat of Hell will reach him." There will be two Angels who will punish him and hit him with huge hammers of fire. Enormous scorpions and snakes will also bite him continuously. Different types of punishments will be meted out to him until the day of Resurrection.

※ ※ ※

DOOMSDAY

A Muslim has to believe that the day and time of everyone's death has been pre-determined. Everything and every living being is mortal. The worlds will come to an end according to the Command of Allah عَزَّوَجَلَّ, Most High, and that will be the Last day, called 'Qiyaamah'.

It is said that the Angel Isrāfeel عَلَيْهِ الصَّلَوةُ وَالسَّلَام, is kneeling beneath the 'Arsh with the trumpet in his hands, waiting for the Command of Allah عَزَّوَجَلَّ, the Most Exalted, to blow it. The first blowing of the Trumpet will bring the world to an end. The earth, the heavens, the Angels and humans – all must perish one day. Only Allah عَزَّوَجَلَّ, Most Exalted, will last forever. But before the world comes to its final end there will appear many signs to herald the nearness of the approaching Doom. Some of these signs are mentioned below:

Disappearance of knowledge

The knowledge of Islam will gradually disappear with the death of Islamic Scholars. There may be some scholars but their minds and hearts will be empty of real knowledge. People will cease to be religiously minded.

Sexual depravity

Sexual depravity will increase. Adultery will become prevalent. Shamelessness will reach such a high level that humans will indulge in sexual intercourse in public like animals. Respect, reverence, etiquette and manners that work as a cementing force for the bonds between young and the old will vanish. The population of males will decrease while that of females will increase. There will be at least fifty women for one man.

False Prophets

People will claim to be Prophets even though Prophethood has ended with Prophet Muhammad صَلَّى اللّٰهُ تَعَالَى عَلَيْهِ وَالِهِ وَسَلَّم. Some of the false prophets that we know of are: Musailama Kazzāb from the Najd Desert of Arabia, Tulaiha Bin Khuwailid, Aswad Ensa, Mirza Ghulam Ahmad Qādiyāni. All of them have made false claims of Prophethood. Others who have not yet appeared will certainly appear one by one before the occurrence of the Day of Judgment.

Abundance of wealth

Wealth will be abundant and visible everywhere, like a mountain of burning coals. This abundance would be so overwhelming it would end up unbearable for the righteous and truthful people who will retire to the graveyards, desiring death.

Time will pass quickly

Time will pass very swiftly, so much so that a year will slip away like a month, a month like a week, a week like a day while a day will fizzle out in a fleeting moment. People will pursue the knowledge of Islam for the sake of their mundane and material needs and not for the sake of Islam itself. Men will be submissive to their women. Children will disobey their parents. Some will prefer to be in the company of their friends and will desert their parents. People will discuss worldly affairs in the Mosques. Music and dance will become the general order of the day. People will curse their ancestors and will talk ill of them. Wild animals will talk to humans. Mean and illiterate people will live in big mansions.

SOME MAJOR SIGNS OF THE HOUR

A.   **The Emergence of Imām Mahdi:** Imām Mahdi رَضِىَ اللّٰهُ تَعَالٰى عَنْهُ is to appear on the scene at a time when Islam vanishes from everywhere and becomes confined within the limits of Hijaaz (Arabia) only. The world will then be full of infidels. In such a

13

compelling and humiliating situation, the Saints (Awliyā) رَحِمَهُمُ اللّٰهُ تَعَالٰی and all the righteous and Allah-Fearing people will leave their respective countries for refuge at the holy cities of Makkah 'the Ennobled' and Madinah 'the Illuminated'.

During the month of Ramaḍān, Imām Mahdi رَضِیَ اللّٰهُ تَعَالٰی عَنْهُ will be amongst the people performing Ṭawaaf around the Holy Ka'bah. The Saints and pious Muslims will recognize him and immediately beseech him to accept their allegiance. Imām Mahdi رَضِیَ اللّٰهُ تَعَالٰی عَنْهُ will first decline their request but will ultimately comply in following a commanding voice from the Unseen, "He is Māhdi, the Khalīfah (vicegerent) of Allah (عَزَّوَجَلَّ). Listen to what he says and follow him." All will then proclaim their faith and allegiance to Imam Mahdi رَضِیَ اللّٰهُ تَعَالٰی عَنْهُ who will lead them to Shaam (Syria).

B. **Emergence of Dajjāl:** Dajjāl, a powerful devilish character will appear on the scene. Besides the Holy cities of Makkah 'the Ennobled' and Madinah 'the Illuminated', he will establish his influence and conquer the entire world in a span of just forty days. The first day of these forty days will be as long as a year. The second day will be like a month and the third day like a week. The rest of the days will be of normal duration. Dajjāl, like a destructive storm will travel around the world, destroying everything in his path. His speed will be like the speed of a cloud carried away by forceful winds. He will unleash destruction wherever he goes. The afflictions and miseries that Dajjāl will cause through his mischief and machinations will be appalling. He will play tricks and display deceptive illusions in order to dupe, misguide, mesmerize and induce the people into following him.

The devious Dajjāl will have two dazzling things with which to entice the people – a garden and a fire. He will call these "Jannah" (Paradise) and "Jahannam" (Hell) and wherever he goes he will take them with him. In reality, in this illusion and magic, his Jannah will actually be fire and his Jahannam will be a peaceful place of rest. He will order people to believe him to be God. Whoever believes him to be God, he will put them into his Jannah, and whoever rejects him, he will throw them into his Jahannam (which will be the opposite).

He will revive the dead and the earth will grow vegetation upon his command. He will make the clouds rain. The livestock of the people during his reign will increase in number and health and the milk-yield will also increase. When Dajjāl passes through the forests, treasures of wealth will follow him like swarms of bees. He will play several other magical tricks and ploys which will ultimately prove to be sheer illusions. All these tricks and ploys will indeed be deceptive feats of magic and wizardry and will instantly vanish as soon as Dajjāl leaves the place. Whenever Dajjāl tries to move towards the holy cities of Makkah and Madinah, Angels will turn his face in some other direction. Dajjāl will be followed by an army of Jews and will have three letters "ك (Kaaf), ف (Faa), ر (Raa)" (signifying Kaafir or disbeliever) engraved on his forehead. Muslims alone will be able to see and read these letters.

15

When Dajjāl completes his round of the world and reaches Syria, it will be dawn. The call to prayer for the morning Ṣalāh would have just finished when the Prophet 'Īsā عَلَى نَبِيِّنَا وَعَلَيْهِ الصَّلٰوةُ وَالسَّلَام will descend onto the eastern minaret of the Jaami' Masjid of Damascus. Imām Mahdi will be present and will be asked by Prophet 'Īsā عَلَى نَبِيِّنَا وَعَلَيْهِ الصَّلٰوةُ وَالسَّلَام to lead the prayer. With the presence of Prophet 'Īsā عَلَى نَبِيِّنَا وَعَلَيْهِ الصَّلٰوةُ وَالسَّلَام this will have a very disastrous effect on Dajjāl who will start melting, like salt in water, due to the fragrance emanating from the breath of Prophet 'Īsā عَلَى نَبِيِّنَا وَعَلَيْهِ الصَّلٰوةُ وَالسَّلَام. This fragrant breath will keep growing in intensity far and wide until Dajjāl is forced to retreat. Prophet 'Īsā عَلَى نَبِيِّنَا وَعَلَيْهِ الصَّلٰوةُ وَالسَّلَام will chase Dajjāl and will finally kill him with a spear.

The end of Dajjāl's domination will mark the beginning of a new era. Prophet 'Īsā's عَلَى نَبِيِّنَا وَعَلَيْهِ الصَّلٰوةُ وَالسَّلَام reign will be one of abundance and affluence. People will be in possession of so much wealth that it will be difficult to find anyone in need of anything. There will be no enmity, jealousy, animosity or distrust among the people. Prophet 'Īsā عَلَى نَبِيِّنَا وَعَلَيْهِ الصَّلٰوةُ وَالسَّلَام will kill the pig (Khinzeer) and break the Cross. All the followers of the Holy Books who survive the tyrannical atrocities of Dajjāl during his regime will eventually proclaim their allegiance to Prophet 'Īsā عَلَى نَبِيِّنَا وَعَلَيْهِ الصَّلٰوةُ وَالسَّلَام. There will now only be one religion – Islam.

C   **The Emergence of Ya'jooj and Ma'jooj ('Gog' and 'Magog'):**
During the magnificent reign of Prophet 'Īsā عَلَى نَبِيِّنَا وَعَلَيْهِ الصَّلٰوةُ وَالسَّلَام, the most powerful tribes from Transoxania named 'Gog' and

'Magog' will appear to commit murder, pillage and plunder wherever they go. They would pass by the lake of Tiberias and drink all of its water. They will then march on till they reach the Mount Khamar in Jerusalem. After the general human massacre, they will try to murder those who are in heaven. Then Prophet 'Īsā عَلَى نَبِيِّنَا وَعَلَيْهِ الصَّلوٰةُ وَالسَّلَام and his companions will pray for help. Allah عَزَّوَجَلَّ, the All-Powerful, will then send insects to destroy Ya'jooj and Ma'jooj. They will be thus killed and their corpses will be taken away by birds.

There will then be profuse rains for many days and consequently the earth will assume the most luxuriant fertility. The period of affluence and prosperity will then be followed by a period of dark days, caused by deep columns of a mysterious smoke. This smoke will appear by the Order of Allah عَزَّوَجَلَّ, Most High, and will engulf the entire globe.

D. **The Appearance of the Dābbatul-Arḍ:** This is an awesome underground creature with a horrible beastly appearance. It will appear menacingly holding in one of its hands the miraculous staff of Prophet Mūsā عَلَى نَبِيِّنَا وَعَلَيْهِ الصَّلوٰةُ وَالسَّلَام and in its other hand the miraculous ring of Prophet Solomon عَلَى نَبِيِّنَا وَعَلَيْهِ الصَّلوٰةُ وَالسَّلَام. With the help of the staff he will make a shining mark on the forehead of every Muslim and with the help of the ring he will put a black mark on the forehead of every disbeliever. These marks will distinguish Muslims from non-Muslims.

E. **The sun rises from the West:** There will then come a time when the sun will rise in the West instead of the East. With this sign becoming evident, the door of repentance will be shut. Allah عَزَّوَجَلَّ, Most Exalted, will now not accept repentance from anyone, nor will anyone be allowed to embrace the faith of Islam.

F. **The Blowing of a Perfumed and Refreshing Wind:** The demise of Prophet 'Īsā عَلَى نَبِيِّنَا وَعَلَيْهِ الصَّلوٰةُ وَالسَّلَام will be followed by a span of forty years after which the Day of Judgment will occur. Towards the end of that period a cool and refreshing wind will blow throughout the world. The sweeping wind will remove the soul of every Muslim from his body, heralding the advent of the Day of Judgment.

The manifestation of the last sign in the form of a mysterious wind will be followed by another spell of forty years during this time no woman will be able to bear children. This will be a period of total disbelief. There will be disbelievers everywhere. There will be no believer left to worship Allah عَزَّوَجَلَّ, Most High.

G. **The blowing of the Trumpet:** Towards the end of that period, Allah عَزَّوَجَلَّ, Most High, will order the Angel Isrāfeel عَلَيْهِ السَّلَام to blow the Ṣoor or the Trumpet. This will mark the beginning of the Day of Judgment. Initially, the sound of the Ṣoor will be mild and gradually it will increase to become intensely loud. At this time people will be busy with their daily chores. On hearing the resounding sound of the Ṣoor, all of them will fall unconscious and die. This deafening sound of the Ṣoor will prove a death-knell for the entire universe. Everything in existence: the earth, heavens, the sun, the moon, stars, mountains, human beings, the Angels including

Isrāfeel عَلَيْهِ السَّلَام and his Ṣoor will vanish into non-existence. There will exist nothing except Allah عَزَّوَجَلَّ, the Almighty. On that day Allah عَزَّوَجَلَّ, the Almighty, will say, "For whom is the Kingdom today?" There will be none to answer. Allah عَزَّوَجَلَّ will then Himself declare, "It is Allah عَزَّوَجَلَّ, the One, the Prevailing."

There will be an interval of forty years between the first and the second blowing of the trumpet. At the first blowing, the world with all its natural phenomena will be destroyed and there will remain nothing but Almighty Allah عَزَّوَجَلَّ. The events that will occur at the time of the first blowing have been described in the Holy Quran:

$$فَاِذَا النُّجُوْمُ طُمِسَتْ ۝$$

$$وَاِذَا السَّمَآءُ فُرِجَتْ ۝ وَاِذَا الْجِبَالُ نُسِفَتْ ۝$$

"So when the stars are extinguished. And when Heaven is split. And when the mountains are blown away as dust." [77: 8-10]

$$فَاِذَا نُفِخَ فِى الصُّوْرِ نَفْخَةٌ وَّاحِدَةٌ ۝ وَّحُمِلَتِ الْاَرْضُ وَالْجِبَالُ فَدُكَّتَا$$

$$دَكَّةً وَّاحِدَةً ۝ فَيَوْمَئِذٍ وَّقَعَتِ الْوَاقِعَةُ ۝ وَانْشَقَّتِ السَّمَآءُ فَهِىَ$$

$$يَوْمَئِذٍ وَّاهِيَةٌ ۝$$

"And when the trumpet is blown instantly. And the earth and the mountains are being crushed after lifting up all at once. That is

the day when the inevitable event will occur. And the heaven will cleave asunder, then on that day it will be in a miserable condition." [69: 13-16]

※ ※ ※

فَإِذَا نُقِرَ فِى النَّاقُورِۙ فَذٰلِكَ يَوْمَىِٕذٍ يَّوْمٌ عَسِيْرٌۙ عَلَى الْكٰفِرِيْنَ غَيْرُ يَسِيْرٍ

"For when the trumpet shall be blown. That day is then a harsh day. For the infidels it is not easy." [74: 8-10]

※ ※ ※

وَنُفِخَ فِى الصُّوْرِ فَصَعِقَ مَنْ فِى السَّمٰوٰتِ وَمَنْ فِى الْاَرْضِ اِلَّا مَنْ شَآءَ اللّٰهُ ؕ ثُمَّ نُفِخَ فِيْهِ اُخْرٰى فَاِذَا هُمْ قِيَامٌ يَّنْظُرُوْنَ

And the trumpet shall be blown, then whoever is in the heavens and whoever is in the earth will collapse but whom Allah (عَزَّوَجَلَّ) wills, then it shall be blown for the second time, henceforth they shall stand looking on." [39:68]

THE REQUIREMENTS OF ISLAM

The five "Pillars" of Islam make up the framework of a Muslim's life, they are:

1. The 'Shahaadah' or Declaration of Faith

To be a Muslim, one must believe in and pronounce the words that mean, "There is no deity worthy of being worshipped except Allah عَزَّوَجَلَّ and Muhammad صَلَّى اللهُ تَعَالَى عَلَيْهِ وَالِهِ وَسَلَّم is His Messenger." This declaration testifies that Almighty Allah عَزَّوَجَلَّ exists, that He is dissimilar and superior to His creation and that none is worthy of worship but Him. It also testifies that He عَزَّوَجَلَّ is the Creator and Owner of all that exists and the Disposer of all affairs. Allah Almighty عَزَّوَجَلَّ says in the Holy Quran:

أَلَا إِنَّ لِلّٰهِ مَنْ فِى السَّمٰوٰتِ وَمَنْ فِى الْاَرْضِ ؕ وَمَا يَتَّبِعُ الَّذِيْنَ يَدْعُوْنَ مِنْ دُوْنِ اللهِ شُرَكَآءَ ؕ اِنْ يَّتَّبِعُوْنَ اِلَّا الظَّنَّ وَاِنْ هُمْ اِلَّا يَخْرُصُوْنَ ۞

Indeed all those in the heavens and all those in the earth are in Allah's control; and what do those who pray to the partners instead of

Allah (عَزَّوَجَلَّ), follow? They do not follow anything except assumption, and they only make guesses. [Yunus 10:66]

The "Shahaadah" is to testify that the Beloved Prophet Muhammad صَلَّى اللهُ تَعَالَى عَلَيْهِ وَاٰلِهِ وَسَلَّم is among the Prophets, who conveyed Almighty Allah's revelation to humankind. Almighty Allah عَزَّوَجَلَّ says:

وَيَقُوْلُوْنَ مَتٰى هٰذَا الْفَتْحُ اِنْ كُنْتُمْ صٰدِقِيْنَ ۝

And they say, "When will this decision take place, if you are truthful?"
[Sajdah 32:28]

In fact, it is stated in the Majestic Quran that the Beloved Prophet Muhammad صَلَّى اللهُ تَعَالَى عَلَيْهِ وَاٰلِهِ وَسَلَّم is the last of Almighty Allah's Messengers. Allah Almighty عَزَّوَجَلَّ says:

مَا كَانَ مُحَمَّدٌ اَبَآ اَحَدٍ مِّنْ رِّجَالِكُمْ وَلٰكِنْ رَّسُوْلَ اللهِ وَخَاتَمَ
النَّبِيّٖنَ ۖ وَكَانَ اللهُ بِكُلِّ شَيْءٍ عَلِيْمًا ۝

Muhammad (صَلَّى اللهُ تَعَالَى عَلَيْهِ وَاٰلِهِ وَسَلَّم) is not the father of any man among you – but he is the Noble Messenger of Allah (عَزَّوَجَلَّ) and the Last of the Prophets[1]; and Allah (عَزَّوَجَلَّ) knows all things. [Ahzab 33:40]

The Holy Quran also confirms that the Beloved and Blessed Prophet Muhammad's صَلَّى اللهُ تَعَالَى عَلَيْهِ وَاٰلِهِ وَسَلَّم words are infallible and

---

[1] Prophet Muhammad صَلَّى اللهُ تَعَالَى عَلَيْهِ وَاٰلِهِ وَسَلَّم is the Last Prophet. There can be no new Prophet after him.

are conveyed from Allah عَزَّوَجَلَّ, the Most Exalted. Almighty Allah عَزَّوَجَلَّ says:

$$وَمَا يَنْطِقُ عَنِ الْهَوٰى ۚ اِنْ هُوَ اِلَّا وَحْیٌ یُّوْحٰى ۙ$$

And he does not say anything by his own desire. It is but a divine revelation, which is revealed to him. [Najm 53:3]

Thus, the Glorious Quran and Sunnah traditions of the Final Prophet Muhammad صَلَّى اللهُ تَعَالٰى عَلَيْهِ وَاٰلِهٖ وَسَلَّم, are the basis of the religion of Islam, and they define every aspect of the Islamic way of life.

# # #

2. The 'Ṣalāh', or the formal 5 times daily obligatory worship

Ṣalāh was practiced in some form or the other throughout history by all Prophets عَلَيْهِمُ الصَّلٰوةُ وَالسَّلَام and their followers as an essential part of Almighty Allah's عَزَّوَجَلَّ religion. Islam, the final message to humanity, considers prayer as crucial. A Muslim is required to pray five times daily within specified periods, as taught by the Beloved Prophet Muhammad صَلَّى اللهُ تَعَالٰى عَلَيْهِ وَاٰلِهٖ وَسَلَّم. These prayers are obligatory, and form a direct bond between the worshipper and his Creator. Islam does not call upon Muslims to merely perform this act of worship; rather; it wants them to purify their souls. Allah عَزَّوَجَلَّ the Most High says, regarding prayer:

أُتْلُ مَا أُوْحِىَ اِلَيْكَ مِنَ الْكِتْبِ وَاَقِمِ الصَّلوةَ ۖ اِنَّ الصَّلوةَ تَنْهٰى عَنِ الْفَحْشَآءِ وَالْمُنْكَرِ ۖ وَلَذِكْرُ اللهِ اَكْبَرُ ۖ وَاللهُ يَعْلَمُ مَا تَصْنَعُوْنَ ۝

O dear Prophet (Muhammad صَلَّى اللهُ تَعَالى عَلَيْهِ وَاٰلِهٖ وَسَلَّم), recite from the Book which has been sent down to you, and establish the prayer; indeed the prayer stops from indecency and evil; and indeed the remembrance of Allah (عَزَّوَجَلَّ) is the greatest; and Allah (عَزَّوَجَلَّ) knows all what you do. [Ankabut 29:45]

3. 'Zakaah,' the obligatory annual poor due

The word 'Zakaah' means purification and growth. An Important principle of Islam is that all things belong to Allah Almighty عَزَّوَجَلَّ. Muslims are enjoined to earn and spend their wealth in ways that are acceptable to Allah عَزَّوَجَلَّ, Most Exalted. The divinely designed system of Zakaah is the right of Almighty Allah عَزَّوَجَلَّ within His Dominion. It is neither a charity nor a tax, but an obligation due from Muslims who possess wealth in excess of their basic needs. Thus, the difference between Zakaah and tax is that a Muslim pays Zakaah willfully and on their own accord; they are the ones who supervise the payment.

Zakaah is only due when a person has the minimum required amount, which varies with the type of wealth. (Daarul Iftā Ahle Sunnat must be contacted for the details of Zakaah, email address: darulifta@dawateislami.net

24

Zakaah cleanses a Muslim of greed, selfishness, and the love of the temporal world. Almighty Allah ﷻ says:

وَالَّذِينَ تَبَوَّؤُا الدَّارَ وَالْإِيمَانَ مِنْ قَبْلِهِمْ يُحِبُّونَ مَنْ هَاجَرَ إِلَيْهِمْ وَلَا يَجِدُونَ فِي صُدُورِهِمْ حَاجَةً مِّمَّا أُوتُوا وَيُؤْثِرُونَ عَلَى أَنْفُسِهِمْ وَلَوْ كَانَ بِهِمْ خَصَاصَةٌ وَمَنْ يُوقَ شُحَّ نَفْسِهِ فَأُولَئِكَ هُمُ الْمُفْلِحُونَ ۝

And those who accepted this city as their home and accepted faith before them, befriend those who migrated towards them, and in their breasts do not find any need for what they have been given, and prefer the migrants above themselves even if they themselves are in dire need; and whoever is saved from the greed of his soul – it is they who are the successful. [Hashr 59:9]

It is the ideal way to meet the needs of the poorer sections of society without causing hardship to the wealthy.

4. 'Ṣiyaam' or fasting

Allah ﷻ the Most Exalted has enjoined fasting upon the Muslims as He had enjoined it upon previous nations. He, the Exalted, says:

يَا أَيُّهَا الَّذِينَ آمَنُوا كُتِبَ عَلَيْكُمُ الصِّيَامُ كَمَا كُتِبَ عَلَى الَّذِينَ مِنْ قَبْلِكُمْ لَعَلَّكُمْ تَتَّقُونَ ۝

O People who Believe! Fasting is made compulsory for you, like it was ordained for those before you, so that you may attain piety.

[Baqarah 2:183]

The Islamic way of fasting involves abstinence from eating, drinking, sexual intercourse and all prohibited habits such as smoking etc. The fast is observed throughout the daylight hours of the lunar month of Ramaḍān (from dawn till sunset). When done in obedience to Almighty Allah's عَزَّوَجَلَّ command fasting teaches believers patience and self-control, as well as reminding them of their responsibility toward the millions of human beings who lack provisions or are victims of their unjust distribution. The month of fasting is accompanied by increased efforts toward good manners and righteous deeds, along with additional worship at night (20 Rak'aat of Tarāweeḥ Ṣalāh). Fasting is not a retreat from life; rather; it is a supplement to the Muslims ordinary activities.

5. 'Hajj' or pilgrimage

Hajj, the annual pilgrimage to Makkah, is a once-in-a-lifetime obligation for those who are physically and financially able to perform it. Almighty Allah عَزَّوَجَلَّ says:

فِيْهِ اٰيٰتٌ بَيِّنٰتٌ مَّقَامُ اِبْرٰهِيْمَ ۖ وَمَنْ دَخَلَهٗ كَانَ اٰمِنًا ۗ وَلِلّٰهِ عَلَى النَّاسِ حِجُّ الْبَيْتِ مَنِ اسْتَطَاعَ اِلَيْهِ سَبِيْلًا ۗ وَمَنْ كَفَرَ فَاِنَّ اللّٰهَ غَنِيٌّ عَنِ الْعٰلَمِيْنَ ﴿٩٧﴾

In it are clear signs - the place where Ibrahim stood (is one of them); and whoever enters it shall be safe; and performing the Hajj (pilgrimage) of this house, for the sake of Allah (عَزَّوَجَلَّ), is a duty upon mankind, for those who can reach it; and whoever disbelieves - then Allah (عَزَّوَجَلَّ) is Independent (Unwanting) of the entire creation! ['Aal-e-'Imran 3:97]

Nevertheless, millions of Muslims journey to the Sanctified city of Makkah each year from every corner of the globe, providing a unique opportunity for people of various nations to meet one another as guests of Allah عَزَّوَجَلَّ, the Most Kind. Hajj is an expression of pure faith and total submission to Almighty Allah's عَزَّوَجَلَّ command, and the pilgrim performs rites of unquestioned obedience, seeking nothing but the acceptance of their efforts and forgiveness of their past sins. A person who has completed the Hajj returns with a fresh outlook on life, a purified soul and blessings from Allah عَزَّوَجَلَّ the Most Kind.

Muhammad صَلَّى ٱللَّهُ عَلَيْهِ وَسَلَّم, the Messenger of Allah

It all began in the year 610 C.E., with a few brave individuals differing in tribe, status and gender, secretly winding through the alleys of Makkah to meet the man known as 'Al-Ameen' (i.e. the trustworthy). One by one they went, stealthily in the moonlight, hoping not to be noticed or reported to powerful city leaders. They were prepared to sacrifice it all – their cultures, families, even their own lives – for the sake of worshipping the One True God (ALLAH عَزَّوَجَلَّ). These fortunate individuals are known as the Sahaabah (Companions of the Beloved Rasool صَلَّى ٱللَّهُ تَعَالَى عَلَيْهِ وَالِهِ وَسَلَّم).

Al-Ameen had called them to cast aside the pagan religion of their forefathers, and to embrace pure monotheism (Towḥeed). The 40-year-old dignified man, whose name was Muhammad (صَلَّى اللهُ تَعَالَى عَلَيْهِ وَآلِهِ وَسَلَّم), claimed that Almighty Allah عَزَّوَجَلَّ regards all people, men and women, free and enslaved, as equal: A message which would, in two short decades, bring peace to the war-torn Arabian Peninsula and beyond; a message forbidding tribal feudalism and corruption by any leader; a message that came to be known as 'Islam', calling for devotion and submission to Allah Almighty (GOD) alone.

⁑ ⁑ ⁑

Who is Muhammad صَلَّى اللهُ عَلَيْهِ وَسَلَّم ?

Prophet Muhammad صَلَّى اللهُ تَعَالَى عَلَيْهِ وَآلِهِ وَسَلَّم was a man of noble descent. He was a model of excellent manners. Allah عَزَّوَجَلَّ, the Most Exalted, praised him by saying:

$$وَ اِنَّكَ لَعَلٰى خُلُقٍ عَظِيْمٍ ۝$$

And indeed you possess an exemplary character. [Qalam 68:4]

Even his enemies attested to his excellent manners. Abū Jahl, who was one of the harshest enemies of Islam, said: "O Muhammad! I do not say that you are a liar! I only deny what you brought and what you call people towards."

Some of his Companions described his manners, saying:

"He (صَلَّى اللهُ تَعَالَى عَلَيْهِ وَآلِهِ وَسَلَّم) was never rough. He never raised his voice in public or used foul language. He did not repay evil with evil; rather, he forgave and pardoned. He did not raise his hand to hit a servant or woman. He would not become angry if he was offended, nor would he take revenge. He only became angry when people transgressed the limits and boundaries of Allah عَزَّوَجَلَّ; in that case he reacted. The Prophet صَلَّى اللهُ تَعَالَى عَلَيْهِ وَآلِهِ وَسَلَّم was not given a choice between two matters, except that he chose the easier of the two, as long as it was not a sinful act. If that act was a sinful act, he would be the furthest from it. When he entered his home he was as normal individual, he would clean his clothes, milk his goats, and serve himself."

From an early age, he had been observed as a thoughtful man. The people of Arabia gave him the title of 'Al-Ameen,' The Faithful/The Trustworthy. A man of truth and fidelity; true in what he did, in what he spoke and thought. They noted that he always meant something. A man who would remain silent when there was nothing to be said; but pertinent, wise, sincere, when he did speak; always throwing light on a matter. This is the only sort of speech worth speaking! Through life we find him to have been regarded as an altogether solid, brotherly, genuine man. A serious, sincere character yet friendly, pleasant, comfortable, always with a radiant smile on his glowing face:

The Beloved Prophet Muhammad صَلَّى اللهُ تَعَالَى عَلَيْهِ وَآلِهِ وَسَلَّم was the most beautiful of people, as his blessed Companions رَضِیَ اللهُ تَعَالَى عَنْهُم, who saw him, informed us. The Beloved and Blessed Prophet Muhammad ﷺ was of a slightly above-average height. Amazingly, in gatherings, he would appear taller than those actually taller than him – until the people dispersed. In complexion, he ﷺ was white with a rosy touch; whitish, but not excessively so. His hair was jet black and wavy, but stopped short of curling, and was kept between his earlobes and shoulders. Sometimes he ﷺ would part his hair at the middle. The Beloved Prophet Muhammad ﷺ had the physique of a powerful man. He ﷺ had a broad upper-back and shoulders, between which was the Seal of Prophethood. He ﷺ had long muscular limbs, large joints and a wide girth. His lean stomach never protruded past the profile of his chest. His face was glowing, "As if the sun was following its course across and shining from his face," His shoulders were broad; he ﷺ was of medium height, neither too tall nor short. He ﷺ was pleasant looking and magnificent; people were full of awe when they saw him for the first time, and knew that his face was not one of a liar.

❉ ❉ ❉

QUESTIONS AND ANSWERS

Regarding the Religion of Islam

1. Who is Allah? 'Do Muslims worship a different God?'

Some people believe that Muslims worship a God that is different from the one worshipped by Christians and Jews. This might be due to the fact that Muslims often refer to God as 'Allah'. This concept is false, since 'ALLAH' is simply the Arabic word for the One true **'Almighty, the Only Worthy of Worship,'** Who created the universe and all humanity. Let there be no doubt – Muslims worship the God of Noah, Abraham, Moses, David, and Jesus عَلَيْهِمُ الصَّلاةُ وَالسَّلامُ. However, it is certainly true that Jews, Christians and Muslims all have different concepts of Almighty God. For example, Muslims – like Jews – reject the Christian belief of the Trinity and the Divine Incarnation. This, however, does not mean that each of these three religions worship a different God – because, as we have already said, there is only One True God. Judaism, Christianity and Islam all claim to be 'Abrahamic Faiths.' However, Islam teaches that other religions have, in one way or another, distorted and nullified a pure and proper belief in Almighty God by neglecting His true teachings and mixing them with man-made ideas.

Arabic speaking people of all religions refer to God as 'Allah.' For example, if you pick up an Arabic translation of the Christian Bible you will see the word 'Allah' where 'God' is used in English. Therefore, 'Allah' is not the God of the Muslims only, but the same God worshipped by all faiths. This idea that 'Allah' is different from 'God' is illogical since it is tantamount to saying that the French worship a different 'God' because they use the word 'Dieu,' and that Spaniards worship a different 'God' because they called him 'Dios', and that the Hebrews worship a different 'God' because they called him 'Yahweh.'

However, the word "ALLAH" is the most suitable name for the Almighty, because it doesn't have a plural form and nor does it have any gender, while the word God has a plural and gender i.e. gods and goddess.

The Glorious Quran, which is the divine scripture of Muslims, was revealed in the Arabic language, so Muslims use the word 'Allah' for 'God,' even when they are speaking other languages. A more literal translation of 'Allah' into English might be *'the one-and-only God'* or *'the one true God.'*

2. The Quran uses the word "We" when quoting Almighty Allah. Does that mean that Muslims believe in more than one God?

Islam adheres to uncompromising and strict monotheism. It teaches that God is One and indivisible. In the Glorious Quran, Almighty Allah عَزَّوَجَلَّ often refers to Himself as "We". But it does not mean that there is more than one God. The reference of Almighty Allah عَزَّوَجَلَّ to Himself as "We" in many Quranic verses is necessarily understood in the Arabic language to denote power and grandeur.

In some languages there are two types of plural forms. One is related to quantity and used to refer to two or more persons, places or things. The other kind of plural is one of majesty, power and distinction. For example, in proper English, the Queen of England refers to herself as "we". This is known as the 'majestic plural or royal plural.'

The oneness of Allah عَزَّوَجَلَّ is stressed throughout the Majestic Quran. A clear example is in this short chapter:

$$قُلْ هُوَ اللّٰهُ اَحَدٌ ۙ اَللّٰهُ الصَّمَدُ ۚ لَمْ يَلِدْ ۙ وَلَمْ يُوْلَدْ ۙ وَلَمْ يَكُنْ لَّهٗ كُفُوًا اَحَدٌ$$

Proclaim (O dear Prophet Muhammad صَلَّى اللّٰهُ تَعَالٰى عَلَيْهِ وَاٰلِهٖ وَسَلَّم), "He is Allah (عَزَّوَجَلَّ), He is One. Allah (عَزَّوَجَلَّ) is Carefree[1]. He has no offspring, nor is He born from anyone. And there is none equal to Him."

[Ikhlas 112:1-4]

3. The Quran says that Almighty Allah is Merciful and that He gives severe punishment. So is He forgiving or is He revengeful?

---

[1] Perfect, does not require anything.

The Majestic Quran mentions many times that Almighty Allah عَزَّوَجَلَّ is the Most Merciful. In fact, all except one of the 114 chapters of the Glorious Quran begins with "بِسْمِ اللهِ الرَّحْمٰنِ الرَّحِيْم", which means,

Allah (عَزَّوَجَلَّ) - beginning with the name of - the Most Gracious, the Most Merciful.

The Compassionate, the Merciful; however in Arabic grammar, both names are intensive forms of the word 'merciful'. Raḥmaan means merciful to all creations, and justice is part of this mercy. Raḥeem means merciful especially to the believers and forgiveness is part of this mercy. A complimentary and comprehensive meaning is intended by the use of both of them together.

In addition, Almighty Allah عَزَّوَجَلَّ speaks of His forgiveness throughout the Glorious Quran. In fact, Almighty Allah's mercy and forgiveness have been mentioned together more than 70 times in the Holy Quran. Allah عَزَّوَجَلَّ, the Most Exalted, repeatedly reminds us by saying:

"And Allah is Forgiving and Merciful."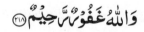

[al-Baqarah 2:218]

But He عَزَّوَجَلَّ also gives severe punishment to those who deserve it. Almighty Allah عَزَّوَجَلَّ told the Beloved and Blessed Prophet Muhammad صَلَّى اللهُ تَعَالٰى عَلَيْهِ وَاٰلِهٖ وَسَلَّم:

نَبِّئْ عِبَادِىٓ اَنِّىٓ اَنَا الْغَفُوْرُ الرَّحِيْمُۙ وَاَنَّ عَذَابِىْ هُوَ الْعَذَابُ الْاَلِيْمُ

34

Inform My bondmen that undoubtedly, I surely am the Oft-Forgiving, the Most Merciful. And that indeed the punishment of Mine is a painful punishment. [Hijr 15:49-50]

Almighty Allah عَزَّوَجَلَّ is 'Just', and His justice necessitates that He rewards those who obey and serve Him and punishes those who disobey and rebel against Him.

If Allah عَزَّوَجَلَّ, the Most Just, punishes a criminal, this would be regarded as His justice and if He forgives a criminal, this would be regarded as his mercy, blessings and forgiveness.

Allah عَزَّوَجَلَّ, the Most Merciful, forgives all those who repent and correct themselves at any stage in their lives, and He has invited all people to His abundant forgiveness and mercy:

قُلْ يٰعِبَادِيَ الَّذِيْنَ اَسْرَفُوْا عَلٰٓى اَنْفُسِهِمْ لَا تَقْنَطُوْا مِنْ رَّحْمَةِ اللّٰهِ ۚ اِنَّ اللّٰهَ يَغْفِرُ الذُّنُوْبَ جَمِيْعًا ۗ اِنَّهٗ هُوَ الْغَفُوْرُ الرَّحِيْمُ ۝ وَاَنِيْبُوْۤا اِلٰى رَبِّكُمْ وَاَسْلِمُوْا لَهٗ مِنْ قَبْلِ اَنْ يَّأْتِيَكُمُ الْعَذَابُ ثُمَّ لَا تُنْصَرُوْنَ ۝ وَاتَّبِعُوْۤا اَحْسَنَ مَاۤ اُنْزِلَ اِلَيْكُمْ مِّنْ رَّبِّكُمْ مِّنْ قَبْلِ اَنْ يَّأْتِيَكُمُ الْعَذَابُ بَغْتَةً وَّاَنْتُمْ لَا تَشْعُرُوْنَ ۝

Proclaim (O dear Prophet Muhammad صَلَّى اللّٰهُ تَعَالٰى عَلَيْهِ وَاٰلِهٖ وَسَلَّم), "O my slaves, who have wronged themselves, do not lose hope in Allah's mercy; indeed Allah (عَزَّوَجَلَّ) forgives all sins; indeed He only is the Oft Forgiving, the Most Merciful." And incline towards your Lord and submit to Him, before the punishment comes to you and then you may not be helped.

And follow this, the best among all, which has been sent down towards you from your Lord, before the punishment comes suddenly upon you whilst you are unaware." [Zumar 39: 53-55]

4. Some believe that Muslims worship Muhammad صَلَّى اللّٰهُ تَعَالَى عَلَيْهِ وَآلِهِ وَسَلَّم. Is this true?

Muslims do not worship Prophet Muhammad صَلَّى اللّٰهُ تَعَالَى عَلَيْهِ وَآلِهِ وَسَلَّم in any way. We believe that he was the last Messenger, the leader of all the Prophets, sent by Almighty Allah عَزَّوَجَلَّ like all His other Prophets and Messengers عَلَيْهِمُ السَّلَام. However, some people mistakenly assume that Muslims worship Prophet Muhammad صَلَّى اللّٰهُ تَعَالَى عَلَيْهِ وَآلِهِ وَسَلَّم.

Prophet Muhammad صَلَّى اللّٰهُ تَعَالَى عَلَيْهِ وَآلِهِ وَسَلَّم, like Jesus عَلَيْهِ السَّلَام, never claimed a divine status. He called people to worship Almighty Allah عَزَّوَجَلَّ alone. Prophet Muhammad صَلَّى اللّٰهُ تَعَالَى عَلَيْهِ وَآلِهِ وَسَلَّم always referred to himself as "Allah's slave and messenger."

Prophet Muhammad صَلَّى اللّٰهُ تَعَالَى عَلَيْهِ وَآلِهِ وَسَلَّم was chosen to be Almighty Allah's عَزَّوَجَلَّ final messenger and to communicate His message to us, not only in words, but also in deeds as a living example of its practical application. Muslims love and respect him because of his impeccable and upright moral character and because he perfectly conveyed the truth from Almighty Allah عَزَّوَجَلَّ and because he is the beloved, chosen and loved by Allah عَزَّوَجَلَّ, the Most Wise – which indeed is the pure monotheism of Islam.

Muslims strive to follow the ideal and great example of the Beloved Prophet Muhammad صَلَّى اللّٰهُ تَعَالَى عَلَيْهِ وَآلِهِ وَسَلَّم, but do not worship him in any way. Islam teaches Muslims to love and respect all of Almighty Allah's Prophets and Messengers عَلَيْهِمُ السَّلَام. However, respecting and loving them does not mean worshipping them. There is a distinct difference between respect and worship. Muslims know that all worship must be directed to Almighty Allah عَزَّوَجَلَّ alone.

In fact, the worship of Prophet Muhammad صَلَّى اللهُ تَعَالَى عَلَيْهِ وَالِهِ وَسَلَّم – or anyone else – along with, or instead of, Almighty Allah عَزَّوَجَلَّ is considered an unpardonable sin in Islam. Even if a person claims to be a Muslim but worships anything other than Allah عَزَّوَجَلَّ, it invalidates ones claim to Islam. The Declaration of faith makes it clear that Muslims must worship Almighty Allah عَزَّوَجَلَّ alone.

5. Is Islam a laid-back religion?

Most Muslims find it rather odd that their religion, which strikes a remarkable balance between faith and deeds, are sometimes accused of being 'laid-back'. Perhaps this misconception came about because Muslims are known to say 'all praise is due to Allah عَزَّوَجَلَّ' whenever anything good or bad happens. This is because Muslims know that everything comes from Almighty Allah عَزَّوَجَلَّ, the Creator of the universe, and occurs by His will. Thus, a Muslim worries less about material matters and views earthly life in the proper perspective. A true Muslim relies completely on Almighty Allah عَزَّوَجَلَّ and knows that whatever happens is always for the best, whether one recognizes it or not, so one graciously accepts whatever cannot be changed.

This does not mean that Muslims should simply await destiny and take no action in life. On the contrary, Islam demands action and effort to change every undesirable situation. To be more precise, action is a required part of one's faith. If human beings did not have the ability to act, it would be unjust to expect them to do and to avoid certain things. Far from being 'laid-back', Islam teaches that man's main obligation in life is to act and exert effort in obedience to Allah عَزَّوَجَلَّ, the All-Powerful.

Islam teaches that human beings should take positive action in this life and supplement it with prayer. Some people are lazy and careless and then blame the negative results on destiny or fate. Some even say that, if Allah عَزَّوَجَلَّ had willed, they would not have sinned or committed crimes. All of these arguments are completely erroneous, because Allah عَزَّوَجَلَّ the Most Wise always does what is right. Almighty Allah عَزَّوَجَلَّ has not ordered us to do anything that we cannot do, because His justice is complete and perfect.

6. Do you believe in life after death and how can you confirm the existence of life after death?

Islam teaches that the present life is a trial in preparation for the next realm of our existence. A day will come when the whole universe will be destroyed and recreated, and the dead will be resurrected to stand in judgment before Almighty Allah عَزَّوَجَلَّ.

The day of Resurrection will be the beginning of another life, one that will be eternal. It is then that every person will be fully compensated by Allah عَزَّوَجَلَّ, the Most Just, for his or her good and evil deeds.

The explanation that the Majestic Quran gives about the necessity of life after death is exactly what the moral consciousness of man demands. If there was no life after death, the very belief in Almighty Allah عَزَّوَجَلَّ would become meaningless, or even if one believed in Him, it would be an unjust and indifferent deity, having once created man and no longer being concerned with his destiny. Surely, Allah عَزَّوَجَلَّ is the Most Just. He will punish the tyrants, whose crimes are beyond count – having killed hundreds of innocent people, created great corruption in the society, enslaved numerous people to serve their own whims and fancies, and so on. Because one has a short life span in this world and since numerous individuals are affected by ones actions, adequate punishments and rewards are impracticable in this life. The Majestic Quran categorically states that the Day of Judgment will come and that Allah Almighty عَزَّوَجَلَّ will decide the fate of each soul.

Each and every human being longs for justice. Even if one does not uphold it for others they want justice for themselves. For example, tyrants and oppressors who are intoxicated by power and influence and inflict pain and suffering on others will object strongly if any injustice is done to them.

Any person who has suffered injustice, irrespective of financial or social status, almost certainly wants its perpetrator to be punished. Though a large number of criminals are punished, many of them get off lightly or are even set free. They may continue to lead pleasant, even luxurious lives and enjoy a peaceful existence. Almighty Allah عَزَّوَجَلَّ may not punish a criminal in this world but He will certainly hold him accountable on the Day of Judgment and punish him.

It is true that a wrongdoer may receive part of the justice that is due to him in this world, but it will remain incomplete. The same is true of someone who deserves great reward and repayments – who had done much good, helped or taught many people, saved lives, suffered to uphold the truth or patiently endured much hardship or injustice. No earthly compensation is adequate for such relentless courage and effort. These types of deeds can only be repaid in full in an eternal life where every individual affected by ones action will testify for or against that person, and where ones innermost thoughts and intentions, known only to Allah عَزَّوَجَلَّ the All-Knowing, will be exposed and judged precisely and perfectly.

Belief in the Hereafter is completely logical. Allah عَزَّوَجَلَّ the Most Exalted has made certain things pleasing and desirable to us in this worldly life, such as justice, although it is usually unattainable. Though a person may obtain a good portion of earthly pleasures and many of his objectives, one remains convinced that the world is unjust. Now, why would the Creator implant in us the love for something we may not experience? The answer is that this life is only one portion of our existence and the Hereafter is the necessary conclusion which balances everything out. Whatever is missing here will be found there; and similarly, whatever is gained unlawfully here will result in deprivation there. That is the perfect and absolute justice that Allah عَزَّوَجَلَّ, the Most Just, has promised.

7. Is it true that Prophet Muhammad صَلَّى اللهُ تَعَالَى عَلَيْهِ وَالِهِ وَسَلَّم wrote the Quran or copied it from the Bible?

In addressing this misconception, it is interesting to note that no other religious scripture claims to totally be the direct word of

Allah عَزَّوَجَلَّ as clearly and as often as the Glorious Quran. Almighty Allah عَزَّوَجَلَّ says:

$$اَفَلَا يَتَدَبَّرُوۡنَ الۡقُرۡاٰنَ ؕ وَلَوۡ كَانَ مِنۡ عِنۡدِ غَيۡرِ اللّٰهِ لَوَجَدُوۡا فِيۡهِ اخۡتِلَافًا كَثِيۡرًا ۝$$

So do they not ponder about the Quran? And had it been from anyone besides Allah (عَزَّوَجَلَّ), they would certainly find much contradiction in it. [Nisa 4:82]

At the time the Glorious Quran was revealed, the Arabs recognized that the language of the Holy Quran was unique and distinctly different from the language spoken by Prophet Muhammad صَلَّى اللهُ تَعَالَى عَلَيۡهِ وَالِهٖ وَسَلَّم and his people. This, in spite of the fact that the Arabs of that time were known for their skills in poetry and mastery of the Arabic language.

Moreover, the Beloved Prophet Muhammad صَلَّى اللهُ تَعَالَى عَلَيۡهِ وَالِهٖ وَسَلَّم was known to be an unlettered man (meaning, that he was not schooled according to the known education system which existed in Arabia at that time, but indeed he صَلَّى اللهُ تَعَالَى عَلَيۡهِ وَالِهٖ وَسَلَّم is taught by Allah عَزَّوَجَلَّ the Most Wise. The Holy Quran states in chapter 4, verse 113 "*And Allah (عَزَّوَجَلَّ) has taught you what you did not know*").

If he went to learn from anyone, certainly his contemporaries would have protested and exposed him. However, there are no reports of this. Without doubt there were people who rejected Prophet Muhammad's صَلَّى اللهُ تَعَالَى عَلَيۡهِ وَالِهٖ وَسَلَّم message, just like the message of other Prophets were rejected, but none denied it for the above mentioned reason.

It is also interesting to note that even though the Majestic Quran is not poetry, the Arabs were much less inclined to poetry after it was revealed. It can be said that the Magnificent Quran is the piece of Arabic literature par excellence – and Prophet Muhammad's صَلَّى اللهُ تَعَالَى عَلَيْهِ وَاٰلِهٖ وَسَلَّم enemies, realized that as much as they tried they could not outdo or even equal it.

Some Christian critics of Islam claim that Muhammad صَلَّى اللهُ تَعَالَى عَلَيْهِ وَاٰلِهٖ وَسَلَّم was not himself the author of the Holy Quran but that he learned and copied (plagiarism) or adapted it from Jewish and Christian scriptures. In reality, however, Prophet Muhammad's صَلَّى اللهُ تَعَالَى عَلَيْهِ وَاٰلِهٖ وَسَلَّم contact with the Jewish and Christian scholars was extremely limited. Historical records available show that he made only three trips outside Makkah before announcing his Prophethood: At the tender age of nine he accompanied his Blessed mother, Lady Aamina رَضِىَ اللهُ تَعَالَى عَنْهَا to Madīnah. Before the age of twelve, he accompanied his uncle Abu Talib on a business trip to Syria. And before his marriage, at the age of 25, he led the honorable Lady Khadījah's رَضِىَ اللهُ تَعَالَى عَنْهَا caravan to Syria.

The most prominent Christian known to him was an old blind man named Waraqah Bin Nawfal, who was a relative of his honorable wife, Lady Khadījah رَضِىَ اللهُ تَعَالَى عَنْهَا. He was a convert to Christianity and well-versed in the gospels. The Beloved Prophet Muhammad صَلَّى اللهُ تَعَالَى عَلَيْهِ وَاٰلِهٖ وَسَلَّم only met him twice; the first time was briefly before his Prophetic mission and the second occasion was when the Beloved Prophet Muhammad صَلَّى اللّٰهُ تَعَالٰى عَلَيْهِ وَاٰلِهٖ وَسَلَّم went to meet Waraqah after receiving the first revelation from Almighty Allah عَزَّوَجَلَّ. Waraqah رَضِىَ اللّٰهُ تَعَالٰى عَنْهُ accepted Islam and was in fact the first Christian scholar to enter into the fold of Islam; he passed away three years later. The revelation of the Glorious Quran, however, continued for 23 years.

Some of Prophet Muhammad's صَلَّى اللّٰهُ تَعَالٰى عَلَيْهِ وَاٰلِهٖ وَسَلَّم pagan opponents accused him of learning the Majestic Quran from a Roman blacksmith, a Christian who was staying on the outskirts of Makkah. A revelation of the Grand Quran was sufficient to refute this charge. Allah Almighty عَزَّوَجَلَّ said:

وَلَقَدۡ نَعۡلَمُ اَنَّهُمۡ يَقُوۡلُوۡنَ اِنَّمَا يُعَلِّمُهٗ بَشَرٌ ؕ لِسَانُ الَّذِىۡ يُلۡحِدُوۡنَ اِلَيۡهِ اَعۡجَمِىٌّ وَّهٰذَا لِسَانٌ عَرَبِىٌّ مُّبِيۡنٌ ۝

And indeed We know that they say, "This Quran is being taught by some other man"; the one they refer to speaks a foreign language, whereas this is clear Arabic! [Nahl 16:103]

Muhammad's صَلَّى اللّٰهُ تَعَالٰى عَلَيْهِ وَاٰلِهٖ وَسَلَّم enemies kept a close watch on him, with the hope of uncovering a shred of evidence to support their claim that he was a liar. But they could not point to a single instance when the Beloved Prophet Muhammad صَلَّى اللّٰهُ تَعَالٰى عَلَيْهِ وَاٰلِهٖ وَسَلَّم might have had a secret meeting with any particular Jew or Christian.

It is true that the Prophet Muhammad صَلَّى اللّٰهُ تَعَالٰى عَلَيْهِ وَاٰلِهٖ وَسَلَّم did have religious discussions with Jews and Christians, but they took place openly in Madīnah, and the revelation of the Glorious Quran had been going on for more than 13 years before that. The allegation that these Jews and Christians were its source is groundless, especially since the role of the Prophet Muhammad ﷺ was of a teacher; he openly invited them to embrace Islam, pointing out how they had deviated from Exalted Allah's ﷻ true teachings of monotheism. Numerous Jews and Christians embraced Islam themselves upon hearing Prophet Muhammad's ﷺ message.

In addition, it was known that Prophet Muhammad ﷺ was unlettered (not taught in any worldly system but taught by Allah ﷻ, the All-Knowing). In His divine wisdom, Allah ﷻ the Most Wise, chose His final messenger to be an unlettered man[1] so no one would have the slightest justification to doubt him or accuse him of writing or copying the Holy Quran. Moreover, there was no Arabic version of the Bible in existence at the time of the Beloved Prophet Muhammad ﷺ.

It is true that there are some similarities between the Majestic Quran and the Bible, but this is not sufficient grounds to accuse the Prophet Muhammad ﷺ of compiling or copying from the Bible. The similarities between the two do not indicate that later Prophets copied from previous ones, but merely point to a common source, who is the one true God, and to the continuation of the basic message of Towḥeed (monotheism).

---

[1] In reality most lettered, taught by Allah ﷻ.

8. How does the Quran differ from other scriptures?

It is an article of faith for every Muslim to believe in all the Prophets and Messengers عَلَيْهِمُ الصَّلوةُ وَالسَّلَام of Almighty Allah عَزَّوَجَلَّ and all unadulterated revelations of God. Some of these scriptures still exist today but not in their pure and pristine form as a result of human alterations. The Majestic Quran is the only divine scripture which has stood the test of time because Allah عَزَّوَجَلَّ the Most Wise has taken the responsibility upon Himself in preserving it. He عَزَّوَجَلَّ, the Exalted says:

$$اِنَّانَحْنُ نَزَّلْنَاالذِّكْرَوَاِنَّالَهُ لَحٰفِظُوْنَ ۞$$

Indeed We have sent down the Quran, and indeed We Ourselves surely are its Guardians. [Hijr 15:9]

Other revealed scriptures[1] before the advent of Prophet Muhammad صَلَّى اللهُ تَعَالٰى عَلَيْهِ وَالِهٖ وَسَلَّم such as the Old Testament and the Gospel, were recorded long after the demise of the Prophets to whom they had been revealed. In contrast, the entire Glorious Quran was written down in its complete form during the lifetime of Prophet Muhammad صَلَّى اللهُ تَعَالٰى عَلَيْهِ وَالِهٖ وَسَلَّم on pieces of palm bark, leather parchment and bone, and arranged in the order designated by the Prophet's Blessed Companions رَضِىَ اللهُ تَعَالٰى عَنْهُم, who committed it to memory and recited it in its original Arabic text, furthermore it continues to be taught and learned by millions of people the world

---

[1] This is one of the miracles of the Quran - no one has been able to change even one letter of its text, despite every effort. It has remained in its original form since the 6th Century (A.C.) and will remain so forever. Other Holy Books such as the Torāh and the Bible have lost their originality.

over. In fact, with every succeeding generation of Muslims, the number of those who commit the whole Holy Quran to memory has incredibly increased. There is no other book, religious or otherwise, which has been given this unparalleled care in recorded history.

The Glorious Quran presents all the Prophets عَلَيْهِمُ الصَّلٰوةُ وَالسَّلَام of Allah Almighty عَزَّوَجَلَّ as belonging to one single brotherhood; all had a similar Prophetic mission and conveyed the same basic message, namely, the invitation to the worship of Allah عَزَّوَجَلَّ alone. The source of their message was one: Allah عَزَّوَجَلَّ (Almighty God). Even if the other scriptures agree with the Magnificent Quran in the fundamental aspects of the religion, they address a specific people. Due to this, its ruling and regulations are particular to them.

On the other hand, the Glorious Quran was revealed to humanity at large and not to any specific nation. Almighty Allah عَزَّوَجَلَّ says:

$$وَمَاۤ اَرۡسَلۡنٰكَ اِلَّا كَآفَّةً لِّلنَّاسِ بَشِيۡرًا$$

$$وَّنَذِيۡرًا وَّلٰكِنَّ اَكۡثَرَ النَّاسِ لَا يَعۡلَمُوۡنَ ۝$$

And O dear Prophet, We have not sent you except with a Prophethood that covers the entire mankind, heralding glad tidings and warnings, but most people do not know [.] *[Saba 34:28]*

[.] Prophet Muhammad صَلَّى اللهُ تَعَالٰى عَلَيۡهِ وَاٰلِهٖ وَسَلَّم is the Prophet towards all mankind.

'Īsā (Jesus) عَلَيْهِ ٱلسَّلَام, the Messenger of Allah عَزَّوَجَلَّ

9. Is it correct that Muslims do not believe in Jesus or other Prophets?

A Muslim cannot be a Muslim if he or she does not believe in Jesus عَلَيْهِ ٱلسَّلَام. Muslims believe in Jesus عَلَيْهِ ٱلسَّلَام and in all of Almighty Allah's Prophets عَلَيْهِمُ ٱلصَّلوةُ وَالسَّلَام. It is a basic element of their faith to believe in all of His Prophets and Messengers عَلَيْهِمُ ٱلصَّلوةُ وَالسَّلَام. Muslims respect and revere Jesus عَلَيْهِ ٱلسَّلَام and awaits his second coming. According to the Magnificent Quran, he was neither crucified nor killed but was raised into Heaven. Muslims consider Jesus عَلَيْهِ ٱلسَّلَام to be among the most prominent Messengers of Allah Almighty عَزَّوَجَلَّ – but not God or the son of God. Jesus' Honorable mother, Lady Mary رَضِىَ ٱللهُ تَعَالَى عَنْهَا is considered a virtuous and noble woman, and the Holy Quran tells us that Jesus عَلَيْهِ ٱلسَّلَام was born miraculously without any father:

$$ اِنَّ مَثَلَ عِيْسٰى عِنْدَ ٱللهِ كَمَثَلِ اٰدَمَ ۘ خَلَقَهٗ مِنْ تُرَابٍ ثُمَّ قَالَ لَهٗ كُنْ فَيَكُوْنُ ۵۹ $$

The example of 'Īsā by Allah (عَزَّوَجَلَّ) is like that of Ādam; He created him (Adam) from clay and then said to him, "Be" - and it thereupon happens! [Aal-e-'Imran 3:59]

Many non-Muslims are surprised to find out that Islam considers, Jesus, the son of Mary, to be one of the greatest messengers of Almighty Allah عَزَّوَجَلَّ. Muslims are taught to love Jesus عَلَيْهِ ٱلسَّلَام, and a person cannot be a Muslim without believing in the virgin birth and in the miracles of Jesus Christ عَلَيْهِالسَّلَامُ. Muslims believe these things about Jesus عَلَيْهِ السَّلَامُ not because of the Bible, but because the Glorious Quran states these things about him. However, Muslims always emphasize that the miracles of Jesus, and of all Prophets عَلَيْهِمُ الصَّلٰوةُ وَالسَّلَامُ, were only possible by "Allah's permission and His Will."

Muslims reject the idea that Allah عَزَّوَجَلَّ, the Most Pure, has a son. The Glorious Quran stresses emphatically that Almighty Allah عَزَّوَجَلَّ 'does not have a son'.

It should be clarified that when Muslims criticize some of the teachings of Christianity, they are not attacking Jesus عَلَيْهِ السَّلَامُ. Christian's doctrines such as the trinity and 'Atonement' are criticized by the Muslims simply because they did not originate from Jesus عَلَيْهِالسَّلَامُ. And when they evaluate the Bible they are not referring to 'God's word' but to writings that are claimed to be God's word.

Muslims believe that the book known today as the Bible only contains bits and pieces of God's original messages, and that it has been tainted by human input and interpolations through numerous revisions and translations. Muslims believe the original Gospel was the words and teachings of Jesus عَلَيْهِالسَّلَامُ, not those of the disciples, Paul or other Church fathers who strongly influenced Christianity throughout history. Islam actually endorses Jesus عَلَيْهِالسَّلَامُ when it insists on the pure monotheism that Jesus عَلَيْهِالسَّلَامُ himself preached and followed.

10. What does the Quran say about Jesus?

Jesus عَلَيْهِ السَّلَام was among the prominent messengers who were mentioned in detail in the Holy Quran. In fact, there is a chapter in the Majestic Quran named Maryam (Mary) رضي اللّٰه تعالى عنها that speaks about the Honorable Lady Mary رضي اللّٰه تعالى عنها and her Blessed son, Jesus عَلَيْهِ السَّلَام. Jesus عَلَيْهِ السَّلَام is also mentioned in various other places throughout the Glorious Quran. Here are some of the Quranic quotations regarding the Honorable Lady Mary عَلَيْهَا السَّلَام رضي اللّٰه تعالى عنها and Jesus:

وَاذْكُرْ فِى الْكِتَابِ مَرْيَمَ ۘ اِذِ انْتَبَذَتْ مِنْ اَهْلِهَا مَكَانًا شَرْقِيًّا ۙ فَاتَّخَذَتْ مِنْ دُوْنِهِمْ حِجَابًا ۠ فَاَرْسَلْنَآ اِلَيْهَا رُوْحَنَا فَتَمَثَّلَ لَهَا بَشَرًا سَوِيًّا ۙ قَالَتْ اِنِّىْٓ اَعُوْذُ بِالرَّحْمٰنِ مِنْكَ اِنْ كُنْتَ تَقِيًّا ۙ قَالَ اِنَّمَآ اَنَا رَسُوْلُ رَبِّكِ ۖ لِاَهَبَ لَكِ غُلٰمًا زَكِيًّا ۙ قَالَتْ اَنّٰى يَكُوْنُ لِىْ غُلٰمٌ وَّلَمْ يَمْسَسْنِىْ بَشَرٌ وَّلَمْ اَكُ بَغِيًّا ۙ قَالَ كَذٰلِكِ ۚ قَالَ رَبُّكِ هُوَ عَلَىَّ هَيِّنٌ ۚ وَلِنَجْعَلَهٗٓ اٰيَةً لِّلنَّاسِ وَرَحْمَةً مِّنَّا ۚ وَكَانَ اَمْرًا مَّقْضِيًّا ۙ فَحَمَلَتْهُ فَانْتَبَذَتْ بِهٖ مَكَانًا قَصِيًّا ۙ فَاَجَآءَهَا الْمَخَاضُ اِلٰى جِذْعِ النَّخْلَةِ ۚ قَالَتْ يٰلَيْتَنِىْ مِتُّ قَبْلَ هٰذَا وَكُنْتُ نَسْيًا مَّنْسِيًّا ۙ فَنَادٰىهَا مِنْ تَحْتِهَآ اَلَّا تَحْزَنِىْ قَدْ جَعَلَ رَبُّكِ تَحْتَكِ سَرِيًّا ۙ وَهُزِّىْٓ اِلَيْكِ بِجِذْعِ النَّخْلَةِ تُسٰقِطْ عَلَيْكِ رُطَبًا جَنِيًّا ۙ فَكُلِىْ وَاشْرَبِىْ وَقَرِّىْ عَيْنًا ۚ فَاِمَّا تَرَيِنَّ مِنَ الْبَشَرِ اَحَدًا ۙ فَقُوْلِىْٓ اِنِّىْ نَذَرْتُ لِلرَّحْمٰنِ صَوْمًا

فَلَنْ أُكَلِّمَ الْيَوْمَ إِنسِيًّا ۝ فَأَتَتْ بِهِ قَوْمَهَا تَحْمِلُهُ ۚ قَالُوا يَمَرْيَمُ لَقَدْ جِئْتِ شَيْئًا فَرِيًّا ۝ يَأُخْتَ هَرُونَ مَا كَانَ أَبُوكِ امْرَأَ سَوْءٍ وَّمَا كَانَتْ أُمُّكِ بَغِيًّا ۝ فَأَشَارَتْ إِلَيْهِ ۖ قَالُوا كَيْفَ نُكَلِّمُ مَن كَانَ فِي الْمَهْدِ صَبِيًّا ۝ قَالَ إِنِّي عَبْدُ اللَّهِ ۖ آتَانِيَ الْكِتَبَ وَجَعَلَنِي نَبِيًّا ۝ وَّجَعَلَنِي مُبَارَكًا أَيْنَ مَا كُنتُ وَأَوْصَنِي بِالصَّلَوٰةِ وَالزَّكَوٰةِ مَا دُمْتُ حَيًّا ۝ وَّبَرًّا بِوَالِدَتِي وَلَمْ يَجْعَلْنِي جَبَّارًا شَقِيًّا ۝ وَالسَّلَمُ عَلَيَّ يَوْمَ وُلِدتُّ وَيَوْمَ أَمُوتُ وَيَوْمَ أُبْعَثُ حَيًّا ۝ ذَلِكَ عِيسَى ابْنُ مَرْيَمَ ۚ قَوْلَ الْحَقِّ الَّذِي فِيهِ يَمْتَرُونَ ۝ مَا كَانَ لِلَّهِ أَن يَتَّخِذَ مِن وَّلَدٍ ۖ سُبْحَنَهُ ۚ إِذَا قَضَى أَمْرًا فَإِنَّمَا يَقُولُ لَهُ كُن فَيَكُونُ ۝ وَإِنَّ اللَّهَ رَبِّي وَرَبُّكُمْ فَاعْبُدُوهُ ۚ هَذَا صِرَاطٌ مُّسْتَقِيمٌ ۝

And remember Maryam in the Book; when she went away from her family to a place towards east. So there she screened herself from them; We therefore sent Our Spirit towards her - he appeared before her in the form of a healthy man[1]. She said, "I seek the refuge of the Most Gracious from you - if you fear God." He said, "I am indeed one sent by your Lord; so that I may give you a chaste son." She said, "How can I bear a son? No man has ever touched me, nor am I of poor conduct!" He said, "So it is; your Lord has said, 'This is easy for Me'; and in order that We make him a sign for mankind and a Mercy from Us; and this

---

[1] Angel Jibrāeel عَلَيْهِ السَّلَام

matter has been decreed." So she conceived him, and she went away with him to a far place. Then the pangs of childbirth brought her to the base of the palm-tree; she said, "Oh, if only had I died before this and had become forgotten, unremembered." (The angel) Therefore called her from below her, "Do not grieve - your Lord has made a river flow below you." And shake the trunk of the palm-tree towards you - ripe fresh dates[1] will fall upon you. Therefore eat and drink and appease your eyes; so if you meet any person then say, 'I have pledged a fast (of silence) to the Most Gracious - I will therefore not speak to any person today.' So carrying him in her arms, she brought him to her people; they said, "O Maryam, you have indeed committed a great evil! O sister of Hāroon, neither was your father an evil man nor was your mother of poor conduct!" Thereupon she pointed towards the child; they said, "How can we speak to an infant who is in the cradle?" The child proclaimed, "I am Allah's bondman; He has given me the Book and made me a Herald of the Hidden (a Prophet). And He has made me blessed wherever I be; and ordained upon me prayer and charity, as long as I live. And has made me good to my mother and not made me forceful, ill-fated. And peace is upon me the day I was born, and on the day I shall taste death, and on the day I will be raised alive. This is 'Isā (Jesus), the son of Maryam; a true statement, in which they doubt. It does not befit Allah (عَزَّوَجَلَّ) to appoint someone as His son - Purity is to Him! When He ordains a matter, He just commands it, "Be" - and it thereupon happens. And said 'Isā, "Indeed Allah (عَزَّوَجَلَّ) is my Lord and your Lord - therefore worship Him; this is the Straight Path." [Maryam 19:16-36]

---

[1] This was a miracle - the date palm was dry and it was winter season.

Islam, science and health matters

11. Is Islam opposed to knowledge and science?

Islam is not opposed to knowledge and science. Knowledge is of two types: religious, which has to do with understanding of the religious duties one is required to carry out, and worldly, which has to do with all that is needed to know with a view to living a comfortable and beneficial life. A Muslim is required to acquire both types of knowledge. In fact, Islam advocated attaining knowledge and education at a time when the whole world was surrounded with darkness and steeped in utter ignorance. The first revelation the Glorious Prophet of Islam (ﷺ) received from Almighty Allah عَزَّوَجَلَّ was:

$$ اِقْرَأْ بِاسْمِ رَبِّكَ الَّذِىْ خَلَقَ ۚ خَلَقَ الْاِنْسَانَ مِنْ عَلَقٍ ۚ اِقْرَأْ وَرَبُّكَ الْاَكْرَمُ ۙ الَّذِىْ عَلَّمَ بِالْقَلَمِ ۙ عَلَّمَ الْاِنْسَانَ مَالَمْ يَعْلَمْ ۙ $$

Read with the name of your Lord Who created. Created man from a clot. Read, and your Lord only is the Most Beneficent, The One Who taught to write with the pen. The One Who taught man all what he did not know. [A'laq 96:1-5]

These verses represent the first spark ever to dispel the darkness of ignorance and barbarianism in which the world had long been engrossed in. And Allah Almighty عَزَّوَجَلَّ reminded the Muslims of His immense favor to humankind, saying:

$$هُوَ الَّذِىْ بَعَثَ فِى الْأُمِّيّنَ رَسُوْلًا مِّنْهُمْ يَتْلُوْا عَلَيْهِمْ اٰيٰتِهٖ وَيُزَكِّيْهِمْ وَيُعَلِّمُهُمُ الْكِتٰبَ وَالْحِكْمَةَ ۚ وَاِنْ كَانُوْا مِنْ قَبْلُ لَفِىْ ضَلٰلٍ مُّبِيْنٍۙ۝$$

It is He Who has sent among the unlettered people a Noble Messenger (صَلَّى اللهُ تَعَالَى عَلَيْهِ وَاٰلِهٖ وَسَلَّم) *from themselves, who recites His verses to them and purifies them, and bestows them the knowledge of the Book and wisdom; and indeed before this, they were in open error. [Jumu`ah 62:2]*

The early generation of Muslims became, in a matter of years, a learned and refined nation in religious as well as worldly matters, after having remained in the darkness of ignorance for centuries. Islam awakened in man the faculty of intellect and motivated him to serve Allah عَزَّوَجَلَّ, the one true God.

Religious knowledge is essential, because, without it, one will not be able to perform his or her obligations in the prescribed manner. Almighty Allah عَزَّوَجَلَّ ordered the Beloved Prophet Muhammad صَلَّى اللهُ تَعَالَى عَلَيْهِ وَاٰلِهٖ وَسَلَّم to pray to Him for advancement of knowledge:

$$وَقُلْ رَّبِّ زِدْنِىْ عِلْمًا۝$$

... and pray, "My Lord, bestow me more knowledge." [Ta-Ha 20:114]

Beneficial worldly knowledge is also necessary, and Muslims are encouraged to acquire it in order to benefit themselves and their fellow humans. When the early Muslims understood this fact, they surpassed other nations in development and productivity and carried the torch of knowledge for many centuries. Islam made great advances in the fields of medicine, mathematics, physics, astronomy, geography, architecture, literature and history, to mention but a few. Many important new procedures such as the use of algebra, Arabic numerals, and the concept of the zero – which was vital to the advancement of mathematics, were transmitted to medieval Europe from Muslim countries. It was the Muslims who developed sophisticated instruments, including the astrolabe, the quadrant and good navigational maps which were to make possible the European voyages of discovery to the New World.

In medicine, mathematics, astronomy, chemistry and physics, Muslims achievements were particularly noteworthy. Well-equipped hospitals, usually associated with medical schools, were located in the principal cities. At a time especially during the 'Dark Ages' of the 'Medieval Times' when superstition still hampered the practice of medicine in western countries, Muslim physicians were diagnosing diseases, prescribing treatments and performing advanced surgery... probably the greatest of all physicians was the 19th century figure, 'Al-Raazi', known in the west as 'Rhazes'. He was the author of numerous scientific works, including a comprehensive medical encyclopaedia and a pioneering handbook on smallpox and measles. A 10th century physician, Avicenna, (Ibn Sīnā) compiled a huge Cannon of Medicine which was considered the standard guide in European medical circles until the late 17th century.... Important advances were made in algebra, analytical geometry and plane spherical trigonometry.

The Glorious Quran itself is a book of guidance and it contains some amazing scientific facts. They are amazing because although they were revealed to the Prophet Muhammad ﷺ over 14 centuries ago, they were not really understood by man until scientists discovered them in very recent times. Although not meant to be a book of scientific facts as such, the Majestic Quran mentions certain realities that would only be recognized and appreciated through technological advancements in later centuries – further undeniable evidence and proof that it was not the work of Prophet Muhammad ﷺ or of any person, but divine revelation of Allah Almighty عَزَّوَجَلَّ.

12. The Quran says that only Allah عَزَّوَجَلَّ knows what is in the womb. Does this not contradict medical science?

To answer this we should look at the verses that relate to this matter. Almighty Allah عَزَّوَجَلَّ says:

إِنَّ اللهَ عِندَهُ عِلْمُ السَّاعَةِ ۖ وَيُنَزِّلُ الْغَيْثَ ۚ وَيَعْلَمُ مَا فِي الْأَرْحَامِ ۖ وَمَا تَدْرِي نَفْسٌ مَّاذَا تَكْسِبُ غَدًا ۖ وَمَا تَدْرِي نَفْسٌ بِأَيِّ أَرْضٍ تَمُوتُ ۚ إِنَّ اللهَ عَلِيمٌ خَبِيرٌ ﴿٣٣﴾

Indeed Allah (عَزَّوَجَلَّ) has the knowledge of the Last Day! And He sends down the rain; and He knows all what is in the mothers' wombs; and no soul knows what it will earn tomorrow; and no soul knows the place where it will die; indeed Allah (عَزَّوَجَلَّ) is the All Knowing, the Informer[1]. [Luqman 31:34]

---

[1] He عَزَّوَجَلَّ may reveal the knowledge to whomever He wills.

And He عَزَّوَجَلَّ says:

اَللّٰهُ يَعْلَمُ مَا تَحْمِلُ كُلُّ أُنْثَىٰ وَمَا تَغِيضُ
الْأَرْحَامُ وَمَا تَزْدَادُ ۖ وَكُلُّ شَيْءٍ عِنْدَهُ بِمِقْدَارٍ ۞

Allah (عَزَّوَجَلَّ) knows all what is inside the womb of every female, and
every increase and decrease of the wombs; and all things are with Him
by a set measure. [Raad 13:8]

If one reads the Arabic text of this verse, they will find that there
is no Arabic word that corresponds to the English word "sex" or
"gender". The Holy Quran mentions only the knowledge of "what"
is in the womb. Many have misunderstood this to mean the gender
of the child in the womb, which is incorrect.

Today, science has indeed advanced, and we can easily determine
the gender of the child in the womb of a pregnant mother using
ultrasound scanning.

Therefore, the above verse refers to every aspect of the fetus'
present and future existence. What will be the child's nature? Will
the child be a blessing or a curse to the parents? What will happen
to him or her throughout life? Will he or she do good or evil? How
long will she or he live? Will he or she end up in Paradise or Hell?
Almighty Allah عَزَّوَجَلَّ alone knows all of this…. no scientist in the
world and no matter how advanced the technology, will ever be
able to determine these things about a child in the mother's womb.

13. The Quran mentions that human beings are created from dust and it also mentions that they are created from sperm. Isn't this contradictory?

Almighty Allah عَزَّوَجَلَّ has said:

$$وَجَعَلْنَا مِنَ الْمَاءِ كُلَّ شَيْءٍ حَيٍّ ط$$

... and we made every living thing from water? [Ambiya 21:30]

And He عَزَّوَجَلَّ said:

$$فَاِنَّا خَلَقْنَاكُمْ مِّنْ تُرَابٍ$$

... then ponder that We created you from dust, [Hajj 22:05]

And He عَزَّوَجَلَّ said:

$$اِنَّا خَلَقْنَاهُمْ مِّنْ طِيْنٍ لَّازِبٍ ۝$$

... We have indeed created them from sticky clay. [Saffat 37:11]

In the preceding verses, Allah عَزَّوَجَلَّ the All-Knowing, has mentioned various stages of human creation. The creation of man according to the Majestic Quran was first from water and dust, which combined and became clay. This refers to the creation of humanity's first ancestor, Prophet Ādam عَلَى نَبِيِّنَا وَعَلَيْهِ الصَّلوةُ وَالسَّلَام. Then Almighty Allah عَزَّوَجَلَّ decreed that his descendants would reproduce after that according to the same natural law that is applied to many other living beings.

Sometimes the Holy Quran refers to semen as "water", meaning fluid. So when Allah Almighty عَزَّوَجَلَّ says in the Glorious Quran that every living thing is from water, it can indicate that everything in creation; humans, animals and plants have all been created from water and depends upon water for their continued existence. But a similar verse: "*And Allah (عَزَّوَجَلَّ) has created every creature from water*[1]" can also mean that human beings and animals are created from their father's semen or sperm. This is confirmed by other verses, such as:

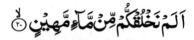

Did We not create you from an abject fluid? [Mursalat 77:20]

As for scientific evidence, research has confirmed that the body of man, like that of other living beings, is made up predominantly of water (about 70% of the human body), and that the elements of the human body are exactly the same as those found in the earth's soil in greater or smaller quantities.

14. Why is the consumption of alcohol prohibited in Islam?

In Islam all things that are harmful or whose harm exceeds their benefits are unlawful. Therefore, alcohol would be deemed unlawful in Islam.

Alcohol has been the curse of human society since time immemorial. It continues to cost countless human lives, and causes misery to millions throughout the world. Statistics showing soaring crime

---

[1] Surah An-Nur, verse 45

rates, increasing instances of mental illnesses and millions of broken homes throughout the world bear witness to the destructive power of alcohol.

Alcohol harms the inhibitory center in the human brain. That is the reason that an intoxicated person is often found to be indulging in behavior that is completely abnormal. A drunkard (euphemistically called a 'problem drinker') finds it difficult to talk or walk properly. He may even urinate in his clothes. If a person should become intoxicated and commits something shameful just once, it may possibly remain with him for the rest of his life.

There are a number of medical reasons for the prohibition of the consumption of alcohol. Millions of people die every year as a result of it. A few of the alcohol related illnesses are:

❖ Cirrhosis of the liver

❖ Various forms of cancer

❖ Esophagitis, gastritis and pancreatitis

❖ Cardiomyopathy, hypertension, angina and heart attacks

❖ Strokes, apoplexy, fits and different types of paralysis

❖ Peripheral neuropathy, cortical atrophy, cerebellar atrophy

❖ Anemia, jaundice and platelet abnormalities

❖ Recurrent chest infections, pneumonia, emphysema and pulmonary tuberculosis

❖ During pregnancy, alcohol consumption has a severe detrimental effect on the fetus, causing 'Fetal alcohol syndrome'.

Many claim that they only have one or two drinks and exercise self-control and so they never get intoxicated. But investigations reveal that every alcoholic started as a social drinker. Not a single drinker drinks with the intention of becoming an alcoholic. It just happens along the way.

The Most Wise Allah عَزَّوَجَلَّ, in His infinite wisdom, made injunctions aimed at preserving the individual and society. Hence the consumption of alcohol is prohibited in Islam. It is worth mentioning that when Muslims refrain from doing things that Almighty Allah عَزَّوَجَلَّ has forbidden, they do not do so because of the harmful effects but because Almighty Allah عَزَّوَجَلَّ has prohibited them. Their aim in this world is to obey Almighty Allah's عَزَّوَجَلَّ commands, and by doing so they also benefit themselves.

Woman in Islam

15. Does Islam oppress women?

In answering this question, we must differentiate between the teachings of Islam and the practice of some Muslims. Although some Muslim cultures oppress women, it often reflects local customs that are inconsistent, if not contrary to Islamic teachings. Islam expects its believers to uphold the rights of women, to protect their social status and prevent their degradation in every way. Islam furthers holds that woman are equal to men in their origin, their humanity, their honor and their accountability before Allah Almighty عَزَّوَجَلَّ.

Today, western societies have actually downgraded women to sex objects. The idea that Islam treats woman as second class citizens worth half a man is nothing but a myth. Islam elevated the status of women over 1,400 years ago by declaring them the sisters of men as believers, giving them the right to education to the highest level, the right to choose a husband, the right to end an unhappy marriage, the right to inheritance, in general, the rights of a full citizen of the state. Not only material and physical rights, but those of kindness and consideration are equally specified and significant in Islamic Law.

Men and women are two equally important component parts of humanity, and the rights and responsibilities of both sexes are equitable and balanced in their totality. Roles of men and women are complementary and collaborative. Although their obligations might differ in certain areas of life in accordance with their basic physical and psychological differences, each is equally accountable for their particular responsibilities.

Under Islamic Law, when a Muslim woman gets married she does not surrender her maiden name, but keeps her distinct identity.

In a Muslim marriage, the groom gives a Mahr (mandatory gift) to the bride herself, and not to her father. This becomes her own personal property to keep, invest or spend, and is not subject to the dictates of any of her male relatives. The Glorious Quran places on men the responsibility of protecting and maintaining all of their female relatives. It means, as well, that a man must provide for his wife and family even if she has wealth of her own. She is not obligated to spend any of her money towards the maintaining of her family. This relieves a woman of the need to earn a living, but she can work if she chooses to do so or if her circumstances warrant it, providing she follows the rules, which the Sharī'ah (Sacred Law of Islam) has prescribed for her in regard to the employment (for further details regarding the conditions of woman's employment, read the book of Ameer-e-Ahle Sunnat Hadrat Moulana Muhammad Ilyas Attar Qadiri 'Parde ke baare Me Suwaal Jawaab').

The family, like any other organization, needs order and leadership. The Majestic Quran states that the husband has a "degree" of authority over his wife, which means guardianship. It is important to note, however, that guardianship is in no way a license to be a tyrant within the household. Rather, it is a burden upon him for his wife and children.

16. Why do Muslim women wear the veil?

The matter of women's dress might seem unimportant to some, especially in today's western societies; however, Islam assigns to it moral, social and legal dimensions. Islam has defined the roles of men and women by allocating certain duties to each and granting certain rights to each. This is in order to maintain a proper balance in society. When men and women observe the proper Islamic dress, they not only protect their own honor and reputation, but they contribute greatly towards peace and order in society.

In general, there are certain guidelines concerning Muslim women's dress. Their garments should not be tight or transparent as to reveal the shape of what is covered. They must cover their entire bodies. This mode of dress is called 'Jilbaab' which refers to a woman's outer garments, with which she is entirely covered. Muslim women do not dress modestly in obedience to their fathers, brothers or husbands, but only in obedience to Allah's عَزَّوَجَلَّ commandments.

Both men and women are expected to be chaste and modest and avoid any type of dress and conduct that may invite temptation. Both are instructed to look only at what is lawful for them to see and to guard their Chastity. Almighty Allah عَزَّوَجَلَّ directs men first and then women in the Magnificent Quran:

قُل لِّلۡمُؤۡمِنِيۡنَ يَغُضُّوۡا مِنۡ أَبۡصَارِهِمۡ وَيَحۡفَظُوۡا فُرُوۡجَهُمۡ ۚ ذٰلِكَ أَزۡكٰى لَهُمۡ ۚ إِنَّ اللّٰهَ خَبِيۡرٌ بِمَا يَصۡنَعُوۡنَ ۝ وَقُلۡ لِّلۡمُؤۡمِنٰتِ يَغۡضُضۡنَ مِنۡ أَبۡصَارِهِنَّ وَيَحۡفَظۡنَ فُرُوۡجَهُنَّ وَلَا يُبۡدِيۡنَ زِيۡنَتَهُنَّ إِلَّا مَا ظَهَرَ مِنۡهَا وَلۡيَضۡرِبۡنَ بِخُمُرِهِنَّ عَلٰى جُيُوۡبِهِنَّ ۖ وَلَا يُبۡدِيۡنَ زِيۡنَتَهُنَّ إِلَّا لِبُعُوۡلَتِهِنَّ أَوۡ اٰبَآئِهِنَّ أَوۡ اٰبَآءِ بُعُوۡلَتِهِنَّ أَوۡ أَبۡنَآئِهِنَّ أَوۡ أَبۡنَآءِ بُعُوۡلَتِهِنَّ أَوۡ إِخۡوَانِهِنَّ أَوۡ بَنِيٓ إِخۡوَانِهِنَّ أَوۡ بَنِيٓ أَخَوٰتِهِنَّ أَوۡ نِسَآئِهِنَّ أَوۡ مَا مَلَكَتۡ أَيۡمَانُهُنَّ أَوِ التّٰبِعِيۡنَ غَيۡرِ أُولِى الۡإِرۡبَةِ مِنَ الرِّجَالِ أَوِ الطِّفۡلِ الَّذِيۡنَ لَمۡ يَظۡهَرُوۡا عَلٰى عَوۡرٰتِ النِّسَآءِ ۖ وَلَا يَضۡرِبۡنَ بِأَرۡجُلِهِنَّ لِيُعۡلَمَ مَا يُخۡفِيۡنَ مِنۡ زِيۡنَتِهِنَّ ۚ وَتُوۡبُوۡا إِلَى اللّٰهِ جَمِيۡعًا أَيُّهَ الۡمُؤۡمِنُوۡنَ لَعَلَّكُمۡ تُفۡلِحُوۡنَ ۝

Command the Muslim men to keep their gaze low and to protect their private organs; that is much purer for them; indeed Allah (عَزَّوَجَلَّ) is Aware of their deeds. And command the Muslim women to keep their gaze low and to protect their chastity, and not to reveal their adornment except what is apparent, and to keep the cover wrapped over their bosoms; and not to reveal their adornment except to their own husbands or fathers or husbands' fathers, or their sons or their husbands' sons, or their brothers or their brothers' sons or sisters' sons, or women of their religion, or the bondwomen they possess, or male servants provided they do not have manliness, or such children who do not know of women's nakedness, and not to stamp their feet on the ground in order that their hidden adornment be known; and O Muslims, all of you turn in repentance together towards Allah (عَزَّوَجَلَّ), in the hope of attaining success[1]. [Noor 24:30-31]

The additional requirements for women to conceal their adornment and natural beauty is due to their greater need for privacy and protection. Except in the company of close relatives, a woman is required to cover her entire body with loose fitting garments.

The Holy Quran states why Almighty Allah عَزَّوَجَلَّ has prescribed particular dress regulations for women:

يَا أَيُّهَا النَّبِيُّ قُل لِّأَزْوَاجِكَ وَبَنَاتِكَ وَنِسَاءِ الْمُؤْمِنِينَ يُدْنِينَ عَلَيْهِنَّ مِن جَلَابِيبِهِنَّ ۚ ذَٰلِكَ أَدْنَىٰ أَن يُعْرَفْنَ فَلَا يُؤْذَيْنَ ۗ وَكَانَ اللهُ غَفُورًا رَّحِيمًا ۝

---

[1] It is incumbent upon women to cover themselves properly.

O Prophet (ﷺ)! Command your wives and your daughters and the women of the Muslims to cover their faces with a part of their cloaks (draw their veils over themselves); this is closer to their being recognised and not being harassed; and Allah is Oft Forgiving, Most Merciful[1]. [Ahzab 33:59]

17. Why does Islam permit polygamy?

Polygamy is a form of marriage wherein a person has more than one spouse. Polygamy can be of two types. The first type is called polygyny, where a man marries more than one woman, and the other is polyandry, where a woman marries more than one man. In Islam, a limited form of polygyny is permitted, whereas polyandry is completely prohibited.

In contrast to Islam, one will not find a limit for the number of wives in the Jewish Talmūd or the Christian Bible. According to these scriptures, there is no limit to how many women a man may marry. Therefore, polygyny is not something exclusive to Islam but was practiced by early Christians and Jews as well. According to the Talmūd, Abraham had three wives, while King Solomon had hundreds of wives. The practice of polygyny continued in Judaism until Rabbi Gershom ben Yehudah (955-1030 CE) issued an edict against it. The Jewish Sephardic communities continued the practice until as late as 1950, when an act of the chief Rabbinate of Israel extended the ban on marrying more than one wife, thus prohibiting the practice for all Jews. In the early teachings of

---

[1] It is incumbent upon women to cover themselves properly.

Christianity, men were permitted to take as many wives as they wished, since the Bible placed no limit on the number of wives, a man could marry. It was only in recent centuries that the Church limited the number of wives to one.

At a time when men were permitted an unlimited number of wives, Islam limited the number to a maximum of four. Before the Holy Quran was revealed, there was no upper limit for polygyny and many men had scores of wives. It gives a man permission to marry two, three or four women, on the strict condition that he deals with all of them equitably, benevolently and justly, as indicated by Almighty Allah's statement:

$$\text{فَإِنْ خِفْتُمْ أَلَّا تَعْدِلُوا فَوَاحِدَةً}$$

... then if you fear that you cannot keep two women equally then marry only one... [Nisa 4:3]

It is not incumbent upon Muslims to practice polygyny. In Islam, taking an additional wife is neither encouraged nor prohibited. Furthermore, a Muslim who has two, three or four wives may not be a better Muslim as compared to a Muslim who has only one wife.

Although it is found in many religious and cultural traditions, polygamy is most often identified with Islam in the minds of westerners. In fact, the Glorious Quran and Islamic Law sought to control and regulate the number of spouses rather than give free license. The Holy Quran allows a man to marry up to four wives, provided he can support and treat them all equally. Muslims regard this Quranic command as strengthening the status of women and the family, for it sought to ensure the welfare of single women and widows in a society whose male population was diminished by warfare, and to curb unrestricted polygamy.

There are certain circumstances which warrant the taking of another wife. For example, if there is a surplus of unmarried women in a society, especially during times of war when widows are in need of shelter and care. Infant mortality rates among males are higher when compared to that of females. During wars, there are usually more men killed than women. The average life span of females is also generally longer than that of males. As a result at any given time in practically any given place, there is a shortage of men in comparison to women. Therefore, even if every single man got married to one woman, there would be millions of women who would still not be able to find a husband.

In western society, it is common for a man to have girlfriends or mistresses, or if he is married, to have extramarital affairs. Seldom is this practice ridiculed, despite the harms that stem from it. At the same time, polygyny is banned in western society although it produces none of these adverse effects; rather it preserves the honor and chastity of women. Within a second, third or fourth marriage the woman is a wife, not a mistress; she has a husband who is obligated by Islamic Law to provide for her and her children, not a 'boyfriend' who may one day cast her aside or deny knowing her if she becomes pregnant.

There is no doubt that a second wife who is lawfully married and treated with honor is better off than a mistress without any legal rights or social respect. Islam strictly prohibits and penalizes prostitution, fornication, and adultery and permits polygyny under strict conditions.

18. If a man is permitted to have more than one wife, then why can't a woman have more than one husband?

Islam teaches that, the Most Wise, Allah عَزَّوَجَلَّ has created men and women as equals, but not as identical beings. They are different, physically, biologically and physiologically and each have different capabilities. Their roles and responsibilities are therefore different but they complement one another.

Some may object to a man having the right to more than one wife by insisting that, in fairness, women should also be able to practice polyandry. However, the following few points could be part of the reason behind its prohibition by Allah Almighty عَزَّوَجَلَّ:

❖ One of the benefits of polygyny is that it solves the problem of women outnumbering men.

❖ In general, men are polygamous by nature while women are not.

❖ Islam assigns great importance to the recognition of parents, both the mother and the father. When a man has more than one wife, the parents of children born in such a marriage can easily be identified. But in the case of a woman marrying more than one husband, only the mother of the children born within the marriage would be known without resorting to laboratory tests. Psychologists tell us that children who do not know their parents, the father in particular, undergo severe mental disturbances and trauma, and often have unhappy childhoods.

19. Why does Islam impose such harsh punishments for sex outside marriage?

Punishment in Islam has a social purpose, which is to dissuade others from committing the same crime. The nature of the punishment depends on the seriousness of the crime in question. Nowadays, some are opposed to the Islamic punishment for fornication and adultery because they see it as unbalanced or too harsh. The basic problem here is the different standards by which the severity of the crime is measured.

Islam views adultery as a very serious crime, because it undermines the very foundation of the family system upon which the whole superstructure of the society is built. Illegitimate relationships destabilize the family and bring about the breakdown of the system. Family breakdown endangers the physical and mental health of future generations, which in turn leads to a vicious circle of corruption, indulgence, and dissolution. Therefore, it is imperative that all measures must be taken to protect the family unit. That is why Islam emphasizes protection of the family by imposing severe punishment for activities that threaten the family foundation. These punishments are the same for men and woman alike.

20. Under Islamic Law, why is a woman's share of inherited wealth half that of a man's?

Islam abolished the former practice whereby inheritance went only to the oldest male heir. According to the Majestic Quran, a woman automatically inherits from her father, husband, her son and her childless brother. The Holy Quran contains specific guidance regarding the division of the inherited wealth amount the rightful beneficiaries. The three verses that broadly describe the share of close relatives are found in Surah an-Nisaa, verse 11, 12 and 176. In these verses, Almighty Allah عَزَّوَجَلَّ establishes the right of children, parents and spouses to inherit a specific share without leaving the matter to human judgment and emotions. In the absence of certain close relatives a share is allocated to more distant ones. The system of inheritance is a perfectly balanced product of the Creator's knowledge of human need and takes into account his imposition of greater responsibility upon particular members of the family in varying situations.

In most cases, the female inherits a share that is half that of the male. However, this is not always so. There are certain instances when they inherit equal shares, and in some cases, a female can inherit a share that is more than that of the male. But even when the male is given a larger share there is a perfectly logical reason behind it. In Islam a woman has no financial obligations towards her family, even if she is wealthy or has her own source of income; the economic responsibility always lies solely upon the man. As long as a woman remains unmarried, it is the legal obligation of her father, brother or other guardians to provide her food, clothing, medication, housing and other financial needs. After she is married, it is the duty of her husband or adult son. Islam holds the man financially responsible for fulfilling all the needs of his family.

So the difference in shares does not mean that one gender is preferred over the other. It represents a just balance between the roles and responsibilities of family members according to their natural physical and emotional makeup. In general, the woman is in charge of running the household and taking care of the needs of those within it, so she is relieved from financial obligations. Despite this, she receives a share of inheritance which becomes her own property to save or use as she pleases. No other person has a claim to any portion of her share. In contrast, the man's share becomes a part of his property from which he is obligated to maintain his children and all female members of the household, so it is constantly being consumed.

Suppose someone died leaving a son and a daughter. The son's share of inheritance will be used up when he gives Mahr (mandatory gift) to his wife and to support his family, including his sister until she marries. Any additional income will have to be earned through work. However, his sister's share remains untouched, or might even increase if she invests it. When she marries, she will receive a Mahr from her husband and will be maintained by him, having no financial responsibilities whatsoever. Thus, a man might conclude that Islam has favored woman over men!

In addition, the Muslim may make a bequest at his own discretion, in which he can make a will to one third of his property to anyone who would not inherit otherwise. The bequest can be a means of assistance to other relatives and people in need, both men and women. One may also allocate this portion or part of it towards charities and good works of his choice.

Islam and terrorism

21. What is Jihad?

While Islam is generally misunderstood in the west, perhaps no other Islamic term suggests such strong reaction as 'Jihad'. The Arabic word 'Jihad' which is mostly mistranslated as 'holy war,' simply means 'to struggle' or 'to exert one's utmost efforts'. It is incorrect to imagine that Jihad is synonymous only with fighting or war, for this is but one particular aspect of the term. Jihad is a struggle to do well and to remove injustice, oppression and evil from oneself and from society. This struggle is spiritual, social, economical and political.

Indeed, the concept of Jihad is one of life, and it is vast, not limited only to armed conflict. For example, one finds in the Glorious Quran, mention of "Jihad by means of the Quran," meaning invitation to the truth, evidence, clarification and presenting the best argument. There is also "Jihad with the soul," which means striving to purify the soul, to increase its faith and incline it towards good, while keeping it from evil and from unlawful desires and temptations. Then there is "Jihad through wealth" which means spending it in various beneficial ways, including charities and welfare projects. And there is "Jihad through the self", which comprises all good works done by a believer, such as propagation, teaching and finally, lawful armed struggle against aggression and oppression.

In the name of Jihad, Islam calls for the protection of societies from oppression, foreign domination and dictatorship that seize rights and freedom, that abolish just and moral rule, that prevent people from hearing the truth or following it, and that practice religious persecution. In the name of Jihad, it endeavors to teach belief in Allah عَزَّوَجَلَّ, the one supreme God, and worship of Him and to spread good values, virtue and morality through wise and proper methods. Almighty Allah عَزَّوَجَلَّ has commanded:

$$ اُدْعُ اِلٰى سَبِيلِ رَبِّكَ بِالْحِكْمَةِ وَالْمَوْعِظَةِ الْحَسَنَةِ وَجَادِلْهُمْ بِالَّتِيْ هِيَ اَحْسَنُ ۚ اِنَّ رَبَّكَ هُوَ اَعْلَمُ بِمَنْ ضَلَّ عَنْ سَبِيْلِهٖ وَهُوَ اَعْلَمُ بِالْمُهْتَدِيْنَ ۝ $$

Call towards the path of your Lord with sound planning and good advice, and debate with them in the best possible way; indeed your Lord well knows him who has strayed from His path, and He well knows the guided. [Nahl 16:125]

In the name of Jihad, Islam calls for social reform and the elimination of ignorance, superstition, poverty, disease and racial discrimination. Among its main goals is the protection of rights for weaker members of society against the imposition of the powerful and influential.

Islam prohibits injustice, even toward those who oppose the religion. Allah ﷻ, the Exalted, says in the Holy Quran:

$$وَلَا يَجْرِمَنَّكُمْ شَنَآنُ قَوْمٍ عَلَىٰٓ أَلَّا تَعْدِلُوا۟ۚ$$

...and do not let the enmity of anyone tempt you not to do justice...
[Maidah 5:8]

And Almighty Allah ﷻ has told the believers regarding those who prevented their entry to the sacred Mosque in Makkah:

$$وَلَا يَجْرِمَنَّكُمْ شَنَآنُ قَوْمٍ أَن صَدُّوكُمْ عَنِ الْمَسْجِدِ الْحَرَامِ أَن تَعْتَدُوا۟ۘ$$

...and let not the enmity of the people who had stopped you from going to the Sacred Mosque tempt you to do injustice... [Maidah 5:2]

Enmity towards any people or nation should not provoke Muslims to commit aggression against them, oppress them or disregard their rights.

One of the highest levels of Jihad is to stand up to a tyrant and speak a word of truth. Restraining the self from wrongdoing is also a great form of Jihad. Another form of Jihad is to take up arms in defense of Islam or a Muslim country when Islam is attacked, but this has to be declared by the Muslim head of a pure Islamic State, who according to Shari'ah conditions, qualifies to become the Khalifah (Caliph).

Although Jihad is a wider concept than just war, it is also clear that Islam acknowledges war when it becomes the last option for the treatment of such problems as oppression and aggression and for the defense of certain freedoms and rights. When Islam acknowledges military engagement, it is an integral part of a complete system of values inherent in the religion, behind which any equitable person can perceive the reason and logic.

War is permissible in Islam only when all peaceful means such as dialogue, negotiations and treaties fail. War is a last resort and should be avoided as much as possible. The purpose of Jihad is not to convert people by force, or to colonize people or to acquire land or wealth or for self-glory. Its purpose is basically the defense of life, property, land, honor and freedom for oneself as well as the defense of others from injustice and oppression.

22. Is Islam a militant religion?

In Islam, the use of force is allowed only in special situations, particularly when the Muslim community is threatened by hostile forces. This is indeed natural and logical for any nation. Then again, the use of force in a campaign of Jihad is determined by the Khalifah (Caliph) of Islamic States in a very ordered and ethical way. Islam considers all life forms as sacred, but particularly emphasizes the sanctity of human life. Allah Almighty عَزَّوَجَلَّ says in the Majestic Quran:

$$وَلَا تَقْتُلُوا النَّفْسَ الَّتِي حَرَّمَ$$
$$اللهُ اِلَّا بِالْحَقِّ ۚ ذٰلِكُمْ وَصّٰكُمْ بِهٖ لَعَلَّكُمْ تَعْقِلُوْنَ ﴿۵﴾$$

... and do not unjustly kill any life which Allah has made sacred; this is the command to you that you may understand [Ana`am 6:151]

Further, Almighty Allah عَزَّوَجَلَّ says:

مَنْ قَتَلَ نَفْسًا بِغَيْرِ نَفْسٍ اَوْ فَسَادٍ فِي الْاَرْضِ فَكَاَنَّمَا قَتَلَ النَّاسَ جَمِيْعًا ط

...whoever kills a human being except in lieu of killing or causing turmoil in the earth, so it shall be as if he had killed all mankind... [Maidah 5:32]

Such is the value of a single human life, that Allah عَزَّوَجَلَّ, the Most Merciful equates the taking of even one human life unjustly as the killing of all of humanity.

It is important to understand that in Islam, war is only permitted in specific and dire circumstances. It is disliked and only permitted as a last resort when all other attempts for peace are unsuccessful. It keeps warfare at a level of mercy and respect for the enemy such as none other has been able to reach. The Beloved Prophet Muhammad صَلَّى اللهُ تَعَالَى عَلَيْهِ وَاٰلِهٖ وَسَلَّم, sometimes had to fight for the mere survival of his mission, but once security was ensured, he immediately reverted to peace and diplomacy.

Even in a state of war, Islam enjoins that Muslim armies, deal justly with the enemy on the battlefield. Islam has drawn a clear line of distinction between the fighters and non-combatants of an enemy country. The Merciful Prophet Muhammad صَلَّى اللهُ تَعَالَى عَلَيْهِ وَاٰلِهٖ وَسَلَّم told his armies:

"Do not kill any old person, any child or any woman." *(Narrated by Abū Dāwood, Hadith no. 2614)*

And he ﷺ said: "Do not kill monks in monasteries." *(Narrated by Ahmad, Hadith no. 2728 – Also in Sharah Ma'ani-al-Athar)*

Upon seeing the corpse of a woman on a battlefield, the Merciful Prophet Muhammad ﷺ angrily asked his companions why she had been killed, and he strongly condemned the awful act. For those enemies active in combat and those taken as prisoners of war, the list of rights is lengthy. There should be no torture; no killing of the wounded or defenseless, no mutilation of enemy bodies and return of enemy corpses must be honored. In light of the aforementioned, it becomes crystal clear that Islam does not permit aggression, violence, injustice, or oppression. At the same time, it calls for morality, justice, tolerance and peace.

Far from being a militant dogma, Islam is a way of life that transcends race and ethnicity. The Grand Quran repeatedly reminds us of our common origin:

يَٰٓأَيُّهَا ٱلنَّاسُ إِنَّا خَلَقْنَٰكُم مِّن ذَكَرٍ وَأُنثَىٰ وَجَعَلْنَٰكُمْ شُعُوبًا وَقَبَآئِلَ لِتَعَارَفُوٓا۟ ۚ إِنَّ أَكْرَمَكُمْ عِندَ ٱللَّهِ أَتْقَىٰكُمْ ۚ إِنَّ ٱللَّهَ عَلِيمٌ خَبِيرٌ ﴿١٣﴾

"O mankind, indeed we created you from male and a female, and made you peoples and tribes that you may know one another. Verily the most noble of you in the sight of Allah (ﷻ) is the most righteous of you." [Hujuraat 49:13]

Schisms between human beings, a world that is currently plagued with terrorism, perpetrated by individuals and by States, Islam is a beacon of light that offers hope for the future.

23. Are Muslims terrorists?

It is very unfortunate that nowadays, Islam has become synonymous with 'terrorism'. Far from promoting terrorism, Islam is a religion of peace whose fundamentals teach its followers to maintain and promote peace and justice throughout the world. Islam does not condone 'terrorism' as defined and understood nowadays: plane hijackings, hostage takings and the torturing and killing of the innocent in order to achieve political or even religious goals. This is not how Islam teaches Muslims to solve their problems, achieve their goals, or to spread their religion.

The question that should be posted instead is: Do the teachings of Islam encourage terrorism? Certainly not, Islam totally prohibits all terrorist acts. It should be remembered that all religions have elements of misguided followers. To be impartial and just, one must consider the teachings of the religion, as they are the yardstick by which the actions of its adherents can be assessed as being right or wrong.

It is completely unfair to judge Islam by the wrongdoings of some misguided or ignorant Muslims, or by the deteriorating condition of Muslims and the blatant corruption that pervades the Muslim world. In fact, what Islam preaches is one thing and what some Muslims nowadays practice is something completely different.

The only way we can do justice to Islam is to find out about its noble teachings, which are clearly set out in the Glorious Quran and Blessed Prophetic traditions.

Islam is a religion of peace, which is acquired by submitting ones will to the Will of the Supreme Creator, Almighty Allah عَزَّوَجَلَّ. Islam promotes peace but at the same time, it exhorts its followers to fight oppression. The fight against oppression may, at times, require the use of force, and sometimes force has to be used to maintain peace. Certainly, Islamic Law allows war under particular circumstances. Any religion or civilization which does not do that, would never survive. But Islam never condones attacks against innocent people, woman or children. Islam also clearly forbids 'taking the law into one's own hands', which means that individual Muslims cannot go around deciding what they want to do by killing or punishing. Trial and punishment must only be carried out by a lawful authority and a qualified judge.

24. How can Islam be called a 'religion of peace' when it was 'spread by the sword'?

It is another common misconception among some non-Muslims that Islam would not have the millions of adherents it has all over the world, had it not been spread by the use of force. The following proofs will make it clear, that far from being forcefully 'spread by the sword,' it was the inherent force of truth, reason and logic that was responsible for the rapid spread of Islam. Islam has always given respect to the freedom of religion to all faiths. Freedom of religion is ordained in the Majestic Quran itself:

لَآ إِكْرَاهَ فِى الدِّيْنِ قَدْ تَّبَيَّنَ الرُّشْدُ مِنَ الْغَيِّ

...There is no compulsion at all in religion; undoubtedly the right path has become very distinct from error... [Baqarah 2:256]

If Islam was indeed spread by the sword, it was the sword of intellect and convincing arguments that was used. It is only this type of sword that conquers the hearts and minds of people. The Glorious Quran says in this connection:

أُدْعُ إِلَى سَبِيْلِ رَبِّكَ بِالْحِكْمَةِ وَالْمَوْعِظَةِ الْحَسَنَةِ وَجَادِلْهُمْ بِالَّتِيْ هِيَ أَحْسَنُ

"Call towards the path of your Lord with sound planning and good advice, and debate with them in the best possible way..." [Nahl 16:125]

The facts speak for themselves

❖ Indonesia is the country that has the largest number of Muslims in the world, and the majority of people in Malaysia are Muslims. But, no Muslim army has ever entered Indonesia or Malaysia. It is an established historical fact that Indonesia entered Islam not due to war, but because of its moral message. Despite the disappearance of Islamic government from many regions once ruled by it, their original inhabitants have remained Muslims. Moreover, they carried the message of truth, inviting others to it as well, and in so doing endured harm, affliction and oppression. The same can be said for those in the regions of Syria and Jordon, Egypt, Iraq, North

America, Asia, the Balkans and in Spain. This shows that the effect of Islam on the population was one of moral conviction, in contrast to occupation by western colonialists, finally compelled to leave lands whose peoples held only memories of affliction, sorrow, subjugation and oppression.

❖ Muslims ruled Spain (Andalusia) for about 800 years. During this period, the Christian and Jews enjoyed freedom to practice their respective religions, and this is a documented historical fact.

❖ Christian and Jewish minorities have survived in the Muslims lands of the Middle East for centuries. Countries such as Egypt, Morocco, Palestine, Lebanon, Syria, and Jordon all have significant Christian and Jewish populations.

❖ Muslims ruled India for about a thousand years, and therefore had the power to force each and every non-Muslim resident of India to convert to Islam, but they did not, and thus more than 80% of the Indian population remains non-Muslim.

❖ Similarly, Islam spread rapidly on the east coast of Africa. And likewise no Muslim army was ever dispatched to the east coast of Africa.

❖ Today, the fastest growing religion in North America, Europe and Africa is Islam. The only sword they have in their possession is the sword of truth. It is this sword that is reverting thousands to Islam.

❖ Islamic Law protects the rights and the status of minorities, and that is why the non-Muslim's places of worship have flourished all over the Islamic world. Islamic Law also allows non-Muslim minorities to set up their own courts, which implement family laws drawn up by the minorities themselves. The life and property of all citizens in an Islamic State are considered important whether they are Muslims or not.

It is clear, therefore, that Islam was not spread by the sword. The often-alleged 'sword of Islam' did not convert all the non–Muslim minorities in Muslims countries. In India, where Muslims ruled for about a thousand years, they are still a minority. In the U.S.A and Canada alone, Islam is the fastest growing religion and has over nine million followers.

25. The Quran says that Muslims should kill the non-believers wherever they find them. Does this mean that Islam promotes violence, bloodshed and brutality?

There are a few verses in the Holy Quran that are quite often misquoted or quoted out of context to perpetuate the myth that Islam promotes violence and exhorts its followers to kill those who are outside the fold of Islam. The words *"kill the polytheists wherever you find them"* are often quoted to portray that Islam promotes violence, bloodshed and brutality.

In order to understand the context, it is necessary to read it from the beginning of the chapter. It discloses that there was a peace treaty between the Muslims and the pagans of Makkah. The pagans violated this treaty, so a period of four months was given to them to make amends; otherwise war would be declared against them. The complete verse actually says:

فَإِذَا انْسَلَخَ الْأَشْهُرُ الْحُرُمُ فَاقْتُلُوا الْمُشْرِكِينَ حَيْثُ وَجَدْتُمُوهُمْ وَخُذُوهُمْ وَاحْصُرُوهُمْ وَاقْعُدُوا لَهُمْ كُلَّ مَرْصَدٍ ۚ فَإِنْ تَابُوا وَأَقَامُوا الصَّلَاةَ وَآتَوُا الزَّكَاةَ فَخَلُّوا سَبِيلَهُمْ ۚ إِنَّ اللَّهَ غَفُورٌ رَّحِيمٌ ۝

Then when the sacred months have passed, slay the polytheists wherever you find them, and catch them and make them captive, and wait in ambush for them at every place; then if they repent and keep the prayer established and pay the charity, leave their way free; indeed Allah (عَزَّوَجَلَّ) is Oft Forgiving, Most Merciful. [Taubah 9:5]

This verse is a command to the Muslims who had entered into an agreement with the pagans, who soon violated the agreement, to fight and kill those who betrayed them wherever they found them. It would seem that any open-minded person would consider the historical context of this verse and agree that it cannot be used as 'evidence' that Islam promotes violence, brutality and bloodshed, or that it encourages its followers to kill anyone outside the fold of Islam.

The very next verse gives the answer to the allegation that Islam promotes violence, brutality and bloodshed. It says:

وَاِنْ اَحَدٌ مِّنَ الْمُشْرِكِيْنَ اسْتَجَارَكَ فَاَجِرْهُ حَتّٰى يَسْمَعَ كَلٰمَ اللّٰهِ ثُمَّ اَبْلِغْهُ مَاْمَنَهٗ ؕ ذٰلِكَ بِاَنَّهُمْ قَوْمٌ لَّا يَعْلَمُوْنَ ۞

And O dear Prophet (Muhammad ﷺ), if a polytheist seeks your protection, give him protection so that he may hear the Word of Allah (عَزَّوَجَلَّ), and then transport him to his place of safety. [Taubah 9:6]

The Holy Quran not only stipulates that a pagan seeking asylum during the battle should be granted refuge, but also that he be escorted to safety. In the present age, which military commander would direct his soldiers not just to spare an enemy during battle, but to escort him to a place of safety? Yet, that is exactly what Almighty Allah عَزَّوَجَلَّ instructs in the Majestic Quran.

Universality of the message of Islam

26. Is it true that Islam is a religion only for Arabs?

This idea can easily be disapproved, as only about 15-20 percent of Muslims in the world are Arabs. There are more Indian Muslims than Arab Muslims, and more Indonesian Muslim than Indian Muslims. This assumption is possibly based on the fact that most of the first generation of Muslims were Arabs, that the Glorious Quran is in Arabic and that the Beloved Prophet Muhammad ﷺ was an Arab.

However, history testifies that the Beloved Prophet Muhammad ﷺ, his followers and the early Muslims made every effort to spread the message of Islam to all nations, races and peoples. From the very beginning of the mission of Prophet Muhammad ﷺ, his followers came from a wide spectrum of countries and races. Among them was Sayyidunā Bilāl, the African slave; Sayyidunā Suhaib, the Byzantine Roman; Sayyidunā 'Abdullāh Bin Salaam, the Jewish Rabbi, and Sayyidunā Salmān Fārsī رَضِىَ اللهُ تَعَالٰى عَنْهُم, the Persian.

Furthermore, it should be clarified that not all Muslims are Arabs and not all Arabs are Muslims. An Arab might be a Muslim, Christian, Jew, atheist or follower of any religion or ideology. Additionally, some countries – such as Turkey and Iran (Persia), that uninformed people consider to be 'Arab' are in fact, not Arab at all. The people who live in those countries speak languages other than Arabic and are of a different ethnic heritage.

Since religious truth is eternal and unchanging, and humanity is considered as one universal brotherhood, Islam teaches that Almighty Allah's عَزَّوَجَلَّ revelations to humanity through the Blessed Prophets عَلَيْهِمُ الصَّلٰوةُ وَالسَّلَام have always been consistent, clear and universal. The truth of Islam is meant for all people regardless of race, nationality, cultural or linguistic background. A brief look at the Muslim world, from Nigeria to Bosnia and from Malaysia to Afghanistan is sufficient proof that Islam offers a universal appeal; a message for all of mankind – not to mention the fact that significant numbers of European and Americans of all races and ethnic backgrounds are finding and entering Islam. The Holy Quran clearly says:

وَمَاۤ اَرۡسَلۡنٰكَ اِلَّا كَآفَّةً لِّلنَّاسِ
بَشِيۡرًا وَّنَذِيۡرًا وَّلٰكِنَّ اَكۡثَرَ النَّاسِ لَا يَعۡلَمُوۡنَ ۞

*And O dear Prophet (ﷺ), We have not sent you except
with a Prophethood that covers the entire mankind, heralding glad
tidings and warnings, but most people do not know. [Saba 34:28]*

27. All religions basically teach their followers to do good deeds, so why should a person follow Islam?

In the Glorious Quran, Almighty Allah عَزَّوَجَلَّ says:

اَلۡيَوۡمَ اَكۡمَلۡتُ لَكُمۡ دِيۡنَكُمۡ
وَاَتۡمَمۡتُ عَلَيۡكُمۡ نِعۡمَتِیۡ وَرَضِيۡتُ لَكُمُ الۡاِسۡلَامَ دِيۡنًا

*...this day have I perfected your religion for you and completed My
favour upon you, and have chosen Islam as your religion...*

[Maidah 5:3]

He عَزَّوَجَلَّ also says:

اِنَّ الدِّيۡنَ عِنۡدَ اللّٰهِ الۡاِسۡلَامُ

Indeed the only true religion in the sight of Allah is Islam...

[Aal-e-'Imran 3:19]

And He عَزَّوَجَلَّ says:

$$وَمَن يَّبْتَغِ غَيْرَ الْإِسْلَامِ دِينًا$$

$$فَلَن يُّقْبَلَ مِنْهُ ۚ وَهُوَ فِي الْآخِرَةِ مِنَ الْخَاسِرِينَ ۞$$

And if one seeks a religion other than Islam, it will never be accepted
from him; and he is among the losers in the Hereafter.

[AaI-e-'Imran 3:85]

Islam is Almighty Allah's عَزَّوَجَلَّ final message, and it offers a complete legal code for humankind. It eliminates and corrects the human errors that have found their way into previous religions in the realm of both belief and practice. Just as any new revised law supersedes and nullifies what came before it, Islam naturally abrogates all earlier religions.

Without a doubt, one will find in every religion, especially those of divine origins, such as Judaism, Christianity and Islam, noble teachings, good moral values, encouragement towards good deeds and warnings against evil. However, what distinguishes Islam from other faiths is that Islam goes beyond simply urging people to be upright and honest. Islam diagnosis illnesses and prescribes the treatment. It gives practical solutions to man's problems and provides the means of achieving righteousness and eliminating evil from individual and collective lives. Islam is guidance for mankind from the All-Wise Creator عَزَّوَجَلَّ Who knows what is best and most suitable for His creation. That is why Islam is called the natural religion of man.

87

A concluding remark

We would now like our readers to ask themselves what they think are the reasons for all the propaganda and misinformation currently being targeted at Islam. If Islam was just another false faith that made no sense, would so many feel a need to invent so many falsehoods about it? The reason is merely that the ultimate truth of Islam stands on unshakable grounds, and that is the basic fundamental belief in the oneness of Almighty Allah عَزَّوَجَلَّ and to believe in the Final Prophet, the Beloved of Allah عَزَّوَجَلَّ, the Leader of all the Prophets, our Master Muhammad Mustafa صَلَّى اللّٰهُ تَعَالٰى عَلَيْهِ وَاٰلِهٖ وَسَلَّم.

Finally, we must never rely on second hand information to understand the religion of Islam. Rather, it needs to be studied from its authentic sources and by speaking to sincere and practicing Muslims.

۞ ۞ ۞

Index

Table of Contents

# # #

# # #